CONSCIOUSNESS
In Transition

Metaphysical Notes

Other Writings of Joel S. Goldsmith

CONSCIOUSNESS
In Transition

Metaphysical Notes

Joel S. Goldsmith

I-Level

Acropolis Books, Publisher

Lakewood, CO   Austell, GA

CONSCIOUSNESS IN TRANSITION
METAPHYSICAL NOTES
FOREWORD AND INTRODUCTION
© 1997 Acropolis Books, Inc.

First Acropolis Books Edition 1997

Published by Acropolis Books, Publisher, under its I-Level Imprint.

For information contact:
Acropolis Books, Inc.
Lakewood, Colorado

http://www.acropolisbooks.com

LIBRARY OF CONGRESS CATALOGING-IN-PUBLICATION DATA

Goldsmith, Joel S. , 1892–1964.
    Consciousness in transition: metaphysical notes/ Joel S.
Goldsmith.
        p.   cm.
    Includes bibliographical references.
    ISBN 1-889051-09-8 (hc : alk. paper)
    1. Metaphysics--Miscellanea. 2. Consciousness--Miscellanea.
3. Spiritual life.   4. Mysticism.   I. Title.
BP610.G6415   1997
299'.93--dc21   97–26457
                                                          CIP

THIS BOOK IS PRINTED ON ACID FREE PAPER THAT MEETS
STANDARD Z 39.48 OF THE AMERICAN NATIONAL STANDARDS INSTITUTE

Except the Lord build the house,
they labour in vain that build it.

—Psalm 127

"Illumination dissolves all material ties and binds
men together with the golden chains of spiritual
understanding; it acknowledges only the leader-
ship of the Christ; it has no ritual or rule but the
divine, impersonal universal Love; no other
worship than the inner Flame that is ever lit at the
shrine of Spirit. This union is the free state of
spiritual brotherhood. The only restraint is the
discipline of Soul; therefore, we know liberty
without license; we are a united universe without
physical limits, a divine service to God without
ceremony or creed. The illumined walk without
fear—by Grace."

— *The Infinite Way* by Joel S. Goldsmith

TABLE OF CONTENTS

TABLE OF CONTENTS

FOREWORD

Consciousness in Transition *is the finest book in today's crop of books encouraging all to develop an awareness of God as ever-present. The author goes further when he says, "If you keep the word of God alive in your consciousness, you will never know lack or limitation."*

Begin to put the words in this book into action and you will learn for yourself that God is truly closer to you than breathing, nearer than hands and feet.

Eileen Bowden

INTRODUCTION

"The words I am speaking clearly show forth the higher consciousness of life. But only as I can reach you within and open your consciousness spiritually can you come into the actual awareness of these words."

– Chapter 8: "Ordination" from *Consciousness In Transition*

In November, 1940, while Joel Goldsmith was First Reader of Third Church of Christ Scientist in Boston, he wrote a note to himself to the effect that his task would be to gather those around him who understood truth as it was presented in his writings. He puzzled over this notation because at that time he had done no writing and had no students. It was not until 1945, after Joel had moved to California, that he began to put into words all that he had come to know as a *way* of life that transcended mere human existence. The results of that writing, a little book called *The Infinite Way*, soon attracted the students that Joel had envisioned so many years before.

Consciousness In Transition, the second in a trilogy of unedited transcripts published by Acropolis Books, brings to life a series of early, "hot off the press," lectures that Joel presented soon after the publication of *The Infinite Way*. Like *Rising In Consciousness*, the first book in the trilogy, *Consciousness In Transition* is a series of lectures given in 1948, in San Francisco, to some of those early students who were coming to Joel requesting instruction. It continues the story of that ground breaking phase in Joel's work which set the foundation for what was to become a worldwide teaching ministry.

The talks Joel was bringing out in San Francisco in 1948 were so stirring that many students began to ask if they could obtain a transcript of each talk, as they wanted to continue working with the class material during the week. The class was recorded on a wire recorder (no high tech recording in those days!) and with Joel's reluctant permission, a secretary volunteered to stay up into the early hours of the morning after each lecture, typing the class so that it would be available to students the following day. These transcriptions were later put into a paper-covered book called *Metaphysical Notes.*

The publication of the 1948 lectures—*Rising In Consciousness* (the San Francisco Lecture Series–1948) and *Consciousness In Transition* (Metaphysical Notes–1948)— saw the fulfilling of the principle ". . . and the Word (the Infinite Invisible) became flesh and dwelt among us. . . ." These early lectures are among the first in which Joel began to publicly lay out a framework of working principles—a framework that was of such integrity and purity that any student of sufficient intent and motivation who worked with the principles would then experience his or her own illumination. *Consciousness In Transition* affords the reader a "you are there" experience of this living message—this living Word—coming into the visible realm.

Since Joel's whole purpose in life was to lift those who came to him into the realization of their own infinite *way*, a way that was always "closer than breathing, nearer than hands and feet," the teacher/student relationship was of utmost importance in his work. So, more than just a book about the Infinite Way principles,

INTRODUCTION

Consciousness In Transition is a fascinating autobiography about the student/teacher relationship—a relationship that was at once inwardly deep and outwardly dynamic.

It is this student/teacher relationship, illuminated so clearly in these lectures, that make this a book as timely now as it was when it was brought out in its original softcover edition in 1949. Why? Because in reading the lectures, in absorbing the principles, we, the readers, are included in the class experience, included in the relatedness.

Indeed, *Consciousness In Transition*, (Metaphysical Notes) allows the reader to sit in on Joel's early classwork, to experience in a measure the intensity of that dedicated group work. In the many lectures Joel gave that year, he covered the practice of meditation, healing and treatment, prayer, the nature of error and God. But more than the comprehensive subject matter, it was the consciousness of the dedicated teacher and deeply motivated students that brought forth the intangible essence of Being that is so evident in a reading of the book. The students who were attracted to the message and who then insisted on instruction, were given the outer message—*and* the inner experience. We, the readers, have the same opportunity.

Laurie Parker
Bellevue, Washington
June, 1997

~ 1 ~

SPIRITUAL HEALING

PREACHING WITHOUT PRACTICE is one of the most deadly of sins, for we must practice what we preach. The first thing that we, as metaphysicians, preach is that without God there is nothing and we exemplify that with: "Except the Lord build the house they labor in vain that build it."[1]

We do not use quotations in this work as quotations, and we must now break the habit of using them as such. You have heard people say, "I do not feel well." Then someone, maybe you, replied, "Oh, no! There is no illness." You did not mean it. You did not know it. They were sick insofar as their sense and yours were concerned. If you had had a consciousness of the truth that they were not sick, you would not have said a word, you would just have smiled. They would have said, "I Am well!" The same with the quotation, "Except the Lord build the house, they labor in vain that build it." A beautiful quotation, but it remains a quotation until you understand it. Here is what I mean by using quotations with understanding. We will start this class with that quotation: "Except the Lord build the house, they labor in vain that build it."

Unless God is the mind of me there will be no truth expressing itself through or as me. Unless God is the

1

mind of you, you will not even understand the truth that is being voiced. Since God is universal mind–since God is my only mind–the only thing that will be voiced in this room is truth expressing itself, God expressing and revealing itself. Since God is the mind of you, God will be revealing itself unto itself. Mind will be expressing its truth unto itself. Truth will not pass from me to you; it will not pass from God to you. The entire activity of truth will take place in the one Mind–the mind of me, which is the mind of you. Why is this the most important part of the entire teaching? Because I expect that from this moment on, every one of you will be called upon to do healing work.

The first thing that you must remember is that you do not have to convey the truth to your patient: "Except the Lord build the house, they labor in vain that build it." If I were to humanly attempt to teach anything, this class would be a failure. If you humanly think that there is some new truth here to be learned, you will be disappointed. There is not a new truth in the entire world. The truth that is to be revealed here has nothing to do with me, for it is not my truth message; it is the word of God that has been imparting itself to universal consciousness throughout all time. It is the word of God which is already embodied in your consciousness. All that is happening tonight is that this truth, which is already your own mind or consciousness, is being consciously unveiled to you–within you.

Please remember, the practical application of this truth is that when you are called upon for help, do not feel that it is necessary to pass truth on to your patient. Any truth that reveals itself within your consciousness instantaneously reveals itself to the consciousness of the person appearing as your patient. You have all seen this in the treatment of cats, dogs and birds. You do not have to tell your animal, your pet, any metaphysical truth. The fact that you know it within your own consciousness makes it evident and manifests instantaneously in the experience of cats, dogs, birds, plants or crops. Become aware of the truth that God, which is the individual mind of this universe, is the one and only mind. All that is necessary is for truth to express itself, to be received in the consciousness of one individual, and it immediately takes effect in the consciousness of all who are attuned. Even if they are not directly your patients, someone in a hospital, someone in a prison, someone on a desert island, someone who is reaching out to his highest concept of God, reaching out for help, can be healed. Though they do not know you or know that you are on this path–and they do not know why they are healed, and you do not know who they are–still it is true, since God is the mind of me and God is the mind of you and there is only that one mind.

None of our work includes the transfer of thought from one individual to another. None of our work is dependent on whether or not the patient understands. None of our work has anything to do with mental suggestion. It has to do with only one thing–realization in the consciousness of the one calling himself practitioner or teacher.

In the three years that the disciples were with Jesus, although they had almost daily contact with him–his thought and his work, he was not able to make much of a spiritual being of Judas, he didn't get too far with Peter, and even less with most of the other disciples. John, of course, caught the full and complete message.

I bring this up for this reason. As you have already seen, this message is a ministry. You are not going to sit through ten lectures. This is a classroom and is entirely different from the lecture room. We are going to bring to light the truth of being but I cannot put it into practice for you. The progress you make will depend on what you make of that which is unfolded and revealed here. It has to be put into practice tonight. You must start in some measure to use what is given in order even to assimilate tomorrow night's lesson.

This is no different from taking a piano lesson. You receive the lesson tonight; if you don't practice it, you will not get any further with another lesson tomorrow night. This is not a course of lectures. If it were, it would be an entirely different thing. You will find that this is a classroom and will be treated as a classroom. The subjects that come up will be taken up as class work and no attempt will be made to make a presentation to you, only to expound, reveal and show forth the practice of this truth. From there on, the degree of your unfoldment will be in the degree of your putting this into practice.

The disciples knew little of Jesus' mission. Jesus had been predicted, prophesied, for centuries. But the Jews thought that the Messiah, when he came (and remember, they expected it to be a man, not a teaching or a divine idea), would lead them into freedom. Freedom from what? Freedom from bondage to Caesar; freedom from being slaves of Caesar; freedom, probably, from some of the wrong practices imposed in their own religion. They were looking for a physical freedom, a temporal freedom. They thought the Messiah would be a king and of course, they were disappointed. The whole of Jesus' mission was not of this world, so the disciples were not ready for it and the Hebrews in the world were not ready for it. No! They were looking for a human emancipator and they failed to understand the mission of the Christ. For that reason, only a few in that day caught the vision and benefitted by it. The rest, regardless of the tribe to which they belonged, have been wanderers on the face of the earth ever since, still seeking economic and political freedom.

Jesus came with the divine idea of spiritual freedom. He hoped that by setting them free in their consciousness from slavery to person and thing, they would be free in fact. But they did not catch the vision.

Now, let no one here mistake the mission of this message. This has nothing to do with a human person called a teacher, but only with the teaching or revelation. It is not primarily concerned with healing physical bodies so that we can have a lot of testimonials: that is not its purpose—nor is its purpose to add ten dollars or a hundred dollars a week to your income. It has nothing to do with temporal improvement; it has to do with the mission of the Christ, which is to set you free spiritually. From what? From your belief in your bondage to person, place, thing, circumstance and condition.

In the ordinary sense of metaphysical healing practice, we seek health as the opposite of disease or as the absence of disease. We think of goodness and morality as the opposite or absence of badness and immorality. In our spiritual unfoldment we are never attempting to heal the body, remove disease, reform sinners, or make good and healthy humans. Our task is the unfoldment and revelation of spiritual being, the harmonious and eternal manifestation of God—good. We are never attempting to change, correct or reform any person. Our work lies within our own being and consists of reaching the spiritual consciousness of Being in which is no temptation to accept the universe and individual being as other than God's being, God appearing as individual being and the universe.

We do not seek health in what Jesus called "this world" because, "My kingdom is not of this world."[2] That is, the Christ work is not in the realm of human concepts. We understand health as the quality and activity of soul that is always expressed as perfect and immortal body. Even a harmonious human body is not necessarily expressing health. Health is more than the absence of disease—health is the eternal state of spiritual being. Human goodness is but the opposite of human badness and is not the spiritual state of being we must realize and achieve in our approach to life.

Our message is not concerned with human health or disease, physical wealth or poverty, personal goodness or badness. Nevertheless, the attainment of the consciousness of God appearing as individual being results in what appears to human sense as health, wealth and goodness. These, however, represent the finite concepts of that which actually is present: spiritual harmony.

When you are no longer in bondage to the belief that you are a slave to some person or circumstance, when you are no longer a slave to dollar bills, you will be truly free forever. Then it will make no difference whether we have a system of capitalism or socialism or communism. You will be abundantly supplied in whatever form of supply is available in the government under which you are living. And, if you are in prison, you will still be free—you will be like those people of old who said, "Imprison me you cannot! Oh, my body you can put in jail, but not me!"

There was a man in prison for a religious offense and under the prevailing form of government he had no opportunity of achieving his physical freedom. So, he practiced the ability of leaving his body at night, wandering out into the world wherever he wanted to go and every morning he came back. Not that it is possible to leave your body, because your body and you are one. But you can leave the corporeal sense of it and be so spiritually free that you are not confined either to time or to space. It is possible, right at this moment, to see one-half of the United States at a glance, while the body sits here in the room. Why? Because mind or consciousness cannot be confined to a room or to a chair; you cannot confine any part of you. The mind can wander around at will and can be trained to so rise above corporeal sense as to actually be out in this world with the sense of being free of the body.

In the outer sense we can say, "I can travel anywhere." But you are not leaving the body—only the corporeal sense of body. That is what happens when you gain your spiritual freedom. You don't stop using dollars, but you are no longer confined to the sense of dollars as supply. You can understand that this undefinable sense, this undefinable essence called spirit or mind or the law of being, is the supply. Then you don't have to worry about the dollars. They will come around.

As long as you have a sense of money as supply, you are not going to demonstrate spiritual freedom or supply. Even if, when this class is over, your income has been doubled, don't congratulate yourself that you have made a demonstration if you still believe that money is supply! You are supply—your consciousness, your life, your mind is supply—and that is omnipresent, omnipotent and omniscient.

Let us begin with what is going to become an important part of our life. In *The Infinite Way*, in the chapter "Meditation," you will find the passage that begins: "On awaking in the morning. . . ." It outlines a course in what you may call mental work or spiritual preparation. I am going to ask you to be very faithful to that, at least throughout the period of this class and as long after as you possibly can.

The first part of our practice is going to be waking up in the morning in the conscious realization of our oneness with God. "Except the Lord build the house, they labor in vain that build it." If you do not bring God—consciously—into your experience right with your first waking moment, you may have lost the opportunity, for quite a while, to have God with you on every occasion.

Right here someone is thinking, "Oh, God is omnipresent, God is always with us!" That is one of those clichés, one of those quotations! Do not believe it because it is not true at all. It is true that God is present, it is true that God is right where you are. But do not believe that is of any benefit to you. You see, if it is true that God is omnipresent, then God must have been present when all of these boys were killed at the front, the Jews put in ovens or of old, the Christians thrown to the lions. What was God doing there while all that was going on? Why was he not helping? God was there, but God is not a person and God cannot look down on you and tell you he is sorry for what you are going through. God is omnipresent in the hospitals, in the prisons, at the front. God is omnipresent. But what good is it to the people, what good is it to you? Only this: in proportion to your *conscious awareness of the presence of God* is God available in every instance.

God is present! Certainly. Electricity was present all through the ages when the people were using whale oil and kerosene oil. What benefit was electricity to them? None. There was no conscious realization of the presence of electricity. Jesus should have been traveling around the holy land in an airplane, too. And the Hebrews on that hike across the sands? It takes forty minutes today, that which took forty years then! The laws of aerodynamics were present and available to them, but they were not consciously aware of the presence of those laws.

You see, there must be a conscious awareness and realization—and really more than that! There must be a conscious feeling of the presence of God in order for you to avail yourself of the presence and power of God. All the rest are only clichés, quotations and hearsay until they become a living reality to you. It is as if you were living back in some ancient time and saying, "You know, electricity is available." That is, if you will hook it up and bring it in.

Talking about God has been going on for thousands of years, and many churches are talking about God and still going through all of the horrors of human experience. The conscious realization of the presence of God is the secret of spiritual living. Once you have contacted God, have had the actual feel or realization of the presence of God, you are no longer alone in the world and no longer working out your own problems and no longer dependent on human aid of any kind. Always, the divine is there.

The Bible says the presence that goes before you is always beside you and comes up behind you as a rearguard. There is such a thing. You would not think so to read the morning accident tables. But, there must be a conscious realization of the presence of God toward that end and toward the development of that state of consciousness we do have certain modes and practices–what we might call human footsteps.

The most important one is learning to awaken in the morning in the conscious realization of the presence of God. If you cannot feel God's presence immediately (and it would not surprise me if you did not), you can at least make the conscious effort to acknowledge the omnipresence, omnipotence and omniscience. You can at least declare and realize:

"As the wave is one with the ocean, so I am one with God.
As the sunbeam is one with the sun so I am one with God. . . ."

If you will take one or two or three minutes to do this, then really and truly, it puts you in a different frame of mind when you step out of bed onto the floor. When you learn not to get out of bed until you have established your conscious oneness with God, you will find your day beginning aright.

When I awaken in the morning, I am in the habit of establishing the conscious realization of the presence of God. I consider that the most important part of my daily work, because, when I have done that, I have not much to do the rest of the day except look over my own shoulder and watch God work.

While we are on the subject, let us not forget that God is *It*. God is not he and not she; God is It. Let us ponder just a while on that subject. Unless we understand God, we will make no progress in this work. Our entire spiritual life depends on our ability to recognize God.

Why is God It, instead of he or she? Firstly, because God is neither male nor female, nor is God a combination of male and female. The Bible says marriages are not given in heaven. There would be, if there were male and female.

Jesus knew God as Father and referred to God as *I*. Abraham knew God as Friend. The great modern Hindu mystic, Ramakrishna, knew God principally as Mother Kali. In ancient Hindu literature, which is the original literature given to the world on the subject of God, God is referred to principally as Mother, sometimes as Father, also as Mind, Principle, Soul, Light, Spirit, or Love. Hindu Scripture is the oldest in the world, dating back thousands of years B.C. and contains all of the known synonyms for God. Because it was the nature of the primitive Hindu, as of the primitive Hebrew, to personalize, they brought God to themselves in the way they understood best—as a loving Mother. For that reason, the most sacred thing the Hindu could call God would be Mother.

We come to the Hebrews and find them, also, a people of intense personal feeling. They personalized God as Friend and as Father. When we come to the Quakers we have the first generally accepted term, that of Father/Mother. Quaker literature, beginning with John Fox in Europe, refers to God as Father/Mother. It so happened that Mrs. Eddy (Mary Baker Eddy) lived eight miles from a Quaker settlement and probably learned this term, Father/Mother, through that connection. Through her, it found its way into Christian Science literature and spread to all metaphysical literature.

As a matter of fact, God is often known as Mother, sometimes as Father, and then as Father/Mother. None

of these terms was meant to mean that God was male or
female; rather that God had both the tender loving and
protective qualities of Mother, and the stern, law-giving,
protective, sustaining and maintaining qualities of Father.
So, when God comes to our individual consciousness, he
comes in such a tender way that we may still use the term
Father or Mother. However, more and more people are
beginning to find God as Light and Life. When God
comes to individual consciousness as Life or as Light,
there is no sense of male or female—just quality.

Well, God is life. God is the universal life that permeates all form. God is the life which permeates your form,
the life which permeates the form of the tree, of the
animal, of the flower. That is impersonal, but it certainly
is life. God is spirit and spirit is the essence of which all
things are formed, all that is in the earth—skies, air,
water—God is the substance, the spirit, the essence, of
which all formation is made.

You may want to know whether this table is God or
God substance. No. It itself is of spirit, but as I see it and
feel it, it represents my concept of God and spirit.
Everything that is out here is God and spirit—everything
in nature, everything in this universe. Everything is
formed of the indestructible and indivisible substance or
spirit that we call God. You say, "Why, then, do we see
rotting trees or volcanoes?" That is not of the essence of
God. That represents our *concept* of that which actually
is here. This is important, because on this point we make
or lose our healing consciousness.

Many have thought that God, spirit, was the actual
substance of the tree, of your body or of the flowers, of
that which you could handle, of any animal or physical
body. But God is not the substance of that. God is the

underlying substance and reality of that, but what you
see, taste, touch or smell, is the product of mortal,
material, finite sense—or the human mind. The sum total
of humans in the world, under what we term medical or
theological law, have set up this finite sense of the
universe which we see, hear, taste, touch and smell.

If you need proof, ask yourself if ever in your life you
have seen or heard or tasted or touched or smelled
anything and later found that it was exactly that way.
Nothing is what it appears to be. We all could be
looking at the same object and every one of us see it
differently. Why? Because we are interpreting it and we
are interpreting it in view of the education and environ-
ment and the background of our individual beings. Now,
God created all that was created and all that he created
is good; therefore this whole world, whether you see it
as humans or animals or plants, is God manifest. But,
when you see it, you do not see it as it is, you see the
finite concept of it.

You are going to hear much more about this, because
that is the one point on which all metaphysical healing
depends and on which ninety-five percent of the failure
is based. Many of our metaphysicians are trying to heal
the physical body—and it can't be healed! There is
nothing you can do to this physical body. When you
change your *concept* of this body, the body responds to
your higher concept, and the person says, "I have been
healed!" He has not. He was perfect to begin with. The
only thing wrong was not in the body, but in the false
concept of himself and of his body.

For that point I am going to refer you to the chapter
"Secret of the Universe" in *Spiritual Interpretation of
Scripture.* Study it carefully. It will save you, right from

the beginning, from making the fatal mistake of trying to heal somebody or somebody's body out there. Take my word for it: you are spiritual now, your body is spiritual now!

When I see your body through my spiritual sense, I behold you as God made you and you will declare that you have been healed. One with truth is a majority. If you will remember, Jacob Boehme of Germany went out and saw through the trees and through the grass to the reality. To mystics it is as though the world opens up and they see the world as God made it. Take my word for it, in the kingdom of God there is never a rotting tree or a beautiful rose destroyed. That is all part of our false conception of God, creation! God's creation is intact; it is perfect, harmonious; it is right here! But I cannot see it with my physical eyes. I can discern it with my spiritual eyes. I can discern it through spiritual sense or through spiritual consciousness. That is what we call Christ-consciousness.

There is no use healing the drunkard of his drinking because he will start all over again. But, if you will look through that individual, you will behold through your spiritual sense the reality of that man. You will bring about that which the world calls healing. Do not try to reform the outer picture. With your inner, God-given spiritual sense, look at the heart and see the Christ. You will find the most wonderful healing force there is in the world. When you meet with thievery or drunkenness or any form of degradation on the street, do not look at it but *through* it. Do not look with the eyes. Close the eyes physically, or at least turn away. Then let your feeling guide you. Get a sense of a feeling of Christ sitting right there in the center of individual being. When you reach that Christ, you will have had an instantaneous healing.

Healings are not brought about through the power of thought, through suggestions or through affirmations or denials. Healings on that basis are like healings with medicines or surgery, as mental power and physical power are the same. Mental power is not spiritual. That will come later.

Right now let us remember that to bring about healing of sin or disease, do not try to set up a human being or body. Get silent within your being. Feel the presence of God, the presence of good. Feel some sort of divine or inner sense. Then you will not think of some individual. You do not have to think of his name or of his form or of his disease. The all-knowing Mind knows. You feel a sense of soul which takes him in. Then you have had a healing. It makes no difference what it is. When the Christ of you touches the Christ of him, there is healing.

Don't try to heal anybody humanly, mentally or physically. Try to get silent in the center of your being and feel the Christ. That is all taking place in the one heart, the heart of God, which is the heart of you. That is why I say we must feel conscious oneness with God. Why? Because God is all-inclusive and since God is all-inclusive, you must be included in that God-being, so that when I am at one with God, I am at one with you. My oneness with God constitutes my oneness with you and with every activity of God that belongs to my life. All of these are divine ideas, the form of which we translate.

Just as your body is a spiritual body in God, neither a male body nor a female body, when you are at the center of your being touching that Christ and that Christ of the individual, there is only pure love, pure spirit.

Because of our human sense, we interpret the qualities of God into both male and female.

So, we may translate the idea of transportation into a donkey or an airplane or a street car or an automobile. These only represent our false concepts of the idea of transportation. The truth about transportation is in one word: instantaneity. *I* am everywhere—here, there and everywhere! That is the truth about spiritual transportation. That is why it is just as easy to sit in San Francisco and heal someone in China as to heal someone right here.

There is only one Life, one Mind, one Soul, but it is still the mind of you and the mind of me. That is why I do not have try to reach out to you. When we are in this conscious oneness, we are so much a part of each other that what you are thinking about truth or God, I am hearing. No mortal thought would get mixed in. We would not receive mortal thinking. In this relationship, we are not one in mortal mind; we are one in Christ, and the only thing we ever get from each other is the divine idea flowing in consciousness.

For that reason you need never worry about malpractice—suffering from other people's thoughts. There is only one mind and that mind is spirit or God. Mortal thinking never goes further than the person in whose thought it takes place. If I were sitting here saying, "Two times two are five," your own mathematical sense would be a protection to you and you would not get my erroneous thought. I could say, "You are dead; you are dead," but your own sense of life would be a protection and you would not be bothered by my illusory thinking. Why? Even in some forms of mental practice experiments have been performed that prove an individual

cannot be made to do anything that violates his own
integrity. They cannot make an honest man steal, and so
on.   They cannot do it because no amount of mortal
thinking can ever make you violate your own integrity.
When you do wrong, it is because you yourself are violating your own sense of right. It lies within your own being.

Now, back to our morning work. Every day, religiously
follow through that entire chapter on meditation and
prayer. For instance, when you leave your house in the
morning do not go out the door without consciously
realizing that the presence has gone before you and the
presence remains behind you to bless those that pass that
way. Do not go out without consciously doing this because
your conscious effort determines your demonstration.

The same way when you eat. Do not eat until you have
at least blinked your eyes and said, "Thank you, Father!"
I am not saying this in any orthodox sense of saying grace.
I am saying it to you in the very modern metaphysical
sense of grace. It is an acknowledgment of God as the
source of your supply, and an acknowledgment that it was
not your own human effort that brought the food to you;
an acknowledgment that of myself I can do nothing, the
Father within me has placed this food before me.

There is no way to jump from being a human being
to being a spiritual being. We can spiritualize our
thoughts little by little until we find ourselves in the
kingdom of heaven. This is how we must begin. We
must learn that regardless of what we are doing through
the day, it is only because of the presence of God that
we are doing it. "Thou wilt keep him in perfect peace
whose mind is stayed on God." Jesus said: "I can of my
own self do nothing; the Father within me doeth the
work."[3] Paul says: "I live, yet not I; Christ liveth in me."[4]

You must see that every bit of good you ever do or experience is the Christ acting in and through you. The good that is in us is the spirit of God activating us.

In conducting your healing practice, be careful that you do not smugly repeat statements of truth to your patients, that you do not give them wonderful quotations of Scripture or of metaphysical writings, unless you yourself have had some measure of consciousness of that truth. Remember, it is far better to say nothing to your patients except, "Leave this with me" or "I will help you" or "I will be with you" or "Call me again in the morning"—far better to give them no truth, merely your assurance that you, with your understanding, are on the job for them. Then, your consciousness is imbued with the spirit of truth, not merely the letter of truth but the spirit of truth, and healing will take place. Then you can explain to your patient what the truth is; then you can give them statements of truth which you have proven, which you have demonstrated, which have become a part of your consciousness. They will not only be glad to hear them, but will feel the truth within them. Giving them quotations and statements of truth of which you yourself have not the consciousness, is really giving a stone when they ask for bread. Rather give them a simple statement, a statement that you have demonstrated over and over—a statement you know to be true—or else, give them the healing silence. Say nothing, but feel within your being this healing Christ.

Remember this. You are not called upon to heal a person. You are not called upon to remove some terrible disease. You are not called upon to change the activity of a human body. All that you are called on to do is to realize the spiritual nature of the omnipresent God and of God's perfect creation. You are called upon to feel—at the center of your being—a living presence.

In every case in which you are called, the real call is for your realization of God as the life of man, God as the mind and the soul and the law and the substance and the cause. Stating these things does not constitute metaphysical practice. It is *feeling* them; it is actual spiritual awareness within your own being.

Now, do not try to reach your patient. Do not try to get your thought across to a patient. Only be sure that within your own being you feel the truth, you feel the rightness, you feel the spiritual sense of being. Your patient will respond. Do not take your patient into your thought—his name or the nature of his disease or what he looks like. Above all, never think that you must convey or transfer some thought from you to your patient. The healing activity is the activity of divine consciousness. It is the activity of the Christ of your own being. It takes place within you.

~ 2 ~

TEACHER AND STUDENT

THE FIRST THING I WANT TO SPEAK ABOUT is the relationship between teacher and student, not only because it will apply to us for a long time, but because it will apply to you and those who come to you for help. I am presenting my idea of the whole of the metaphysical subject. My essential presentation is that the relationship between teacher and student is a very sacred one; it is a relationship not built or dependent on any degree of human knowledge a person called a teacher has, because that amount of knowledge will be of little benefit to a student. What a student gets from a teacher is the spiritual integrity of the teacher. That is what transmits itself, and without that there is nothing to transmit.

Words can be found in books, and libraries are filled with books. If they could take the place of a teacher, there would be no other teaching than books. But there is something that books cannot convey that an individual can. That is spiritual integrity or spiritual consciousness. It is up to a teacher or practitioner, then, to maintain spiritual integrity. By that I mean living up to his own teaching or his own understanding or his highest sense of his own teaching or his own understanding.

No one, of course, could live any higher than his understanding, but it is possible to sink lower than that.

It is possible to violate one's own integrity, to know the spiritual truth and not live up to it. It is a case of, "if you preach it, you are teaching it." On the other hand, if you are living up to your highest sense of your spiritual integrity, and if you never say a word to your student or patient, he will receive illumination. That is really spiritual law. In the same way, a teacher must feel an obligation to stand by the student as long as there is a need for it. There must always be that willingness and readiness to reach out and give him whatever his need may be, in the form of an interview, telephone calls, or letters.

Understand, it is your student's or patient's responsibility not to make a nuisance of himself, to keep his requirements and demands on a legitimate plane. As long as the teacher maintains spiritual integrity, the student should stand by the teacher. If the teacher falls from grace, the student should stand by with the teacher and lift him up until it has become evident that the teacher does not want to be lifted up. Then the student should find his own way and form his own path to heaven. Also, a teacher should stand by with his student if he falls from grace until the student makes it clear he does not want the help of the teacher and has no intention of changing his ways. Then the teacher should feel free to sever that relationship.

The teacher at all times must be making it evident that the object of teaching is to set the student free of the teacher. That is the main object of spiritual teaching. Unless that happens, you have a repetition of what happened with Jesus and his disciples when he finally had to say to them, "If I go not away, the Comforter will not come to you ."[1]

A lecturer, in talking, quoted: "To those leaning on the sustaining Infinite, they should not lean too often and too long!" The teacher must be careful not to encourage the student to live at the teacher's feet. The object of spiritual teaching is to set the student free of the teacher, to set him free in his own Christhood. That is the idea as I see it. All who have ever been in class with me are perfectly free to call on me at any time for help to lift them to a place where they become independent and are able to walk on the water themselves.

"My sheep hear my voice."[2] Only those on this particular level of consciousness will be drawn to this message. The teaching is as ancient as ancient days, but is presented to you as given by Christ Jesus. It represents my understanding of spiritual law and truth as revealed by Krishna, Shankara, Jesus of Nazareth, and the beloved disciple, John. Its foundation is oneness, the oneness of God and man: "I and the Father are one." The message stands literally on the First Commandment: There is but one power, one presence, one life, one mind, soul, or spirit–and this truth is the principle of individual being.

We find God as the only substance of creation, as the law and substance of all form. And we understand that what we behold with the five physical senses is but the human or limited concept of that which actually is there. We know that even a good or healthy appearance is but the false sense of the reality; that we can never see or hear God's creation physically, but can, with spiritual sense, discern the man and universe of God's unfoldment of its own being, called "creation."

The world does not accept one power. It gives power to climate, germs, food, stars and countless other effects.

Understand that no effect of itself is or has power. Mind–life, truth–is the power unto every effect.

This revelation of God–one presence and one power–came to King Amenhotep IV of Egypt from India. He took from his people their many gods and replaced these with one. Eventually Amenhotep was deposed, the many gods restored, and Abraham, a close friend of the king, fled to Ur of the Chaldees. There, Abraham taught the one God and became father of the Hebrew people.

Shankara of India again gives the teaching in its fullness and simplicity as the Advaita teaching of India. In it, Shankara reveals the nature of God as the "I" or "I Am," the oneness of God and man which he sums up as "I Am that." He also reveals the illusory nature of the sense world. Then comes Jesus of Nazareth with the sublime message and demonstration of oneness, of "I and the Father are one,"[3] that evil is not real. He proves by his healing of the sick, raising from the dead, feeding the multitudes, and finally, in his own rising above all sense testimony into the revelation of the truth, "I am eternal life." Again, this present age is presenting the ancient wisdom and "with signs following" in the form of healed and regenerated men and women. Briefly, then, we summarize: God and man is one–and not two; "I and the Father are one. . . . All that the Father hath is mine[4] . . . All that God is, I am."

On the positive side, the teaching has for its foundation that every individual individualizes all of the qualities and activities of God. Every individual individualizes all intelligence, eternal life, all love, all truth. Not one bit is left out of any individual. Also, that the very oneness of the individual with the universal constitutes the oneness of the individual with every God-created being and idea in the world. That is the positive side, or positive half of this teaching.

The other half, which I make equal with the understanding of the nature of God, is the individual's relationship to the nature of error. I do that for this reason: In our daily experience we are faced with problems of our own or of the world or of others' coming to us for help. Unless we perceive the unreal nature of what is appearing to us as error, as sin, as disease, lack, war, etc. we cannot handle it scientifically and thus reverse the picture. We may fall into blind faith healing, which is neither good nor permanent. We would not have a problem if there was not something producing that problem in our experience. We say, "The problem is not real. I know it is not real." What good is it to know it is not real if it is still going to keep annoying us as if it were?

We must come to a place in consciousness where we know what to do with this nothingness called evil; how to overcome, dispel, get free of it. It is nothing. That is true. The metaphysical revelation of the nature of error is true—it is nothing! But it remains a problem until we have really come into the *awareness* which makes it nothing in our experience. So the second half in this teaching relates to the nature of error and what to do about it.

Now, let us say that the teaching is composed of the letter of truth and the spirit of truth. The letter of truth has two parts: first, the nature of God and the relationship of God and man; and second, the nature of error, and what to do about it. That is all there is to this teaching so far as the letter of truth is concerned. We have absolutely no observances of any kind—no rites, no ritual, no dogma. We have no formulas, no approaches.

Nothing more nor less than that understanding of God and of the nature of error, and your own individual application of it.

I follow by saying that the letter of truth is the least important part of this teaching. The only necessity for it is to keep you free of the danger of falling into a blind faith teaching, to keep you from some blinding faith that somewhere, somehow, there is a God doing something. It is necessary to have the correct letter of truth and to learn its application as a basis. We leave it very quickly and go into the actual spirit of truth, and that is the most important part of this work. Whether you see it as an ever-present Father or Law or Mother or Guide or Support, the spirit of truth—gaining the actual conscious- ness of the presence of God, gaining an actual contact with God, gaining the actual realization of God as an ever-presence—depends on your own individual make- up. But God is ever-present, and while we are actually the individualization of all that God is, nevertheless, as humans, this God-being seems to be something separate and apart from us until it makes itself known within our consciousness as the reality of our own being. That is the purpose of this teaching.

In the teaching of Jesus I have found authority for this. It is true I have found the same teaching all the way back to the Eastern teachings of three and four thousand B.C., but in no case so clearly stated, so clearly demon- strated, as in the case of Jesus. Therefore, while I love to read about these other approaches, there is no other approach that is quite as definite, quite as complete, quite as easy for us to accept, because it is really part of our Western consciousness. I can find authority for practically everything that I teach in the New Testament.

As a matter of fact, almost all of it is found in the Gospel according to John and in the writings of Paul.

Actually, there are only three absolute teachings in the world and those three come under the unfoldment or revelation of Buddha, Shankara and Jesus. Buddha's teaching has been completely lost in the church, or the many churches which now call themselves Buddhist. As a matter of fact, it would be as difficult to find Buddha's original teaching in Buddhism, as to find any tracing of Jesus' teaching in any Christian church. In many cases they actually and openly deny his teaching: where in the churches do we find the teaching of praying for the enemy? Which church in World War I or II held prayer services for the enemy? Which taught the soldiers to pray daily for those who were persecuted? Who taught the members of congregations that those who live by the sword must die by the sword? Who revealed the spiritual point in Jesus' refusal to let Peter avenge him by cutting off the ear of the Roman soldier? Who taught the Commandment: "Thou shalt not kill."[5]? Only the development of spiritual consciousness will finally enable all nations to put up the sword and turn them into ploughshares.

When we are talking about the teaching of Jesus, we are not talking about the teaching of Jesus as presented through any of the recognized churches, but as found in the New Testament, without anybody's opinion, without anybody's interpretation—just taking literally Jesus' teachings. You might ask, "Can we live up to it?" You would find very quickly that it can be done. You can live up to it as an individual, and if you can, the world can. The world probably is not ready for it but you are, and you can live up to it. You can take your position of

forgiving the enemy, of praying for those that persecute
you. You can, because there is a metaphysical way that
makes it possible. So if this teaching is to be named at
any time, the only name that can be given to it is the
teaching of Jesus Christ as it is in the New Testament.

There can be no doubt that we owe our greatest debt
to the Christian Science Church for its metaphysics,
because there we were given the method of applying
truth to our human problems. Now, the method that was
applied in original treatment is not the method I am
speaking of, although that was the foundation out of
which the rest has grown. In my own case I was doing
healing work and was in the practice two years before I
knew anything about Christian Science treatment. And
then I learned about it and learned there are things in it
that are necessary to know, and those things are known
in all of the metaphysical movements. It so happens that
I owe my debt to the Christian Science movement
because I learned treatment work there.

I say that we are not actually teaching any of these
teachings, and that is true. We are teaching this: You
must individually contact God. God must become as real
and alive to you in your individual experience as I am
real to you sitting up here. That is the purpose of this
entire work, raising consciousness to that point: "I, if I be
lifted up, will draw all men nigh unto me."[6] And the
moment that I make the contact and feel the presence of
God, in that moment everyone who is within range of
that consciousness must feel it and be lifted up. Ultimately they are lifted up to that degree where they make
contact themselves and have the realization themselves.
That is the purpose of this work.

So for a moment now, let me review this. If there is a
secret, or a secret teaching about this, it can be briefly

summed up: In the degree that you can open your consciousness to the inflow of the presence of God, or the Christ, in that degree do you practice. In the degree that your consciousness is open to the awareness of God, in that degree do you ultimately demonstrate it. The ultimate demonstration was voiced both by Jesus and by Paul. Jesus said: "I of mine own self can do nothing, the Father within doeth the works."[7] And I do not mean there were two people—Jesus and the Father. I recognize that when he used the term Father he meant the divine Essence or Presence or Law of the infinite. That is what he meant by the Father, and so do we. In acknowledging God, or a divine Father, we are not acknowledging some person or even some being or power outside ourselves. That would be two-ness, that would be duality—and that would be fatal.

We acknowledge that, "I am the only One. I and my Father are One, and I am that One. But this thing that I feel coursing through me, that is the Father and it is greater than I, greater than the humanhood." Paul voiced it: "I live, yet not I; the Christ liveth in me."[8] He was not thinking of a man named Jesus living "in me," or some kind of separate being living in him. He knew he meant the Christ, the Messiah, the Savior, the Essence, the Power, the Law, the Presence. True, it has the strength and power and dominion of a father, the love and tenderness of a mother, the understanding of a friend. But it is a presence that cannot be defined.

That is where our troubles come in with language. Lao-Tzu said: "If you can define it, it is not God." If you ever could describe this thing, you would not be describing God, because God is infinity, eternality, immortality—and you cannot describe it. You can feel it, become conscious of it, aware of it, that which is the central theme of this teaching.

This is not another metaphysical approach to get rid of disease, to demonstrate an automobile or health. This really is a willingness to take no thought for your life, for the things that you eat or drink or wherewithal you shall be clothed. It is an attempt to seek the consciousness of God and let these things be added. You could not possibly have the consciousness of God and some kind of lack, the consciousness of infinity and an absence of something. So, in attaining the consciousness of the presence of God, you likewise attain all the added things, all those things which are in and of God.

Now, another step in this teaching which makes it a little bit radical, and very simple once you catch it, is that it is a teaching of one power. We do not use truth to overcome error. We do not use the power of God to overcome evil. We stand on the platform of the First Commandment: "Thou shalt have no other powers but me."[9] There are no other powers but God. There is no sin to overcome, no death, no lack, no limitation, no temptation. The only power, the only presence, is God. When belief says to us in the form of sin, disease, death, lack, limitation, "I have power to crucify you," we have the same smile Jesus wore when he said: "Thou couldest have no power unless it came to you from the Father, which is in heaven."[10] That treatment he was giving to Pilate was a statement of absolute truth, and he turned around and proved it, because with all of Pilate's power to nail him to the cross, he could not touch Jesus' life. So Pilate's power was an empty one. It was nothingness. And so with us. Our stand is on the First Commandment.

Get to know my writings on the Ten Commandments in *Spiritual Interpretation of Scripture* and see how clearly the light of the one power is revealed all the way through. Give up this idea that truth dispels error. Error is not a reality and does not have to be destroyed—it merely has to be recognized for the nothingness that it is. God, Truth is the only power. We do not use it. We *are* it. That which I am seeking—I *am*.

Early in my practice I had a call. A lady had help from many practitioners and teachers but they got nowhere with her. She was paralytic. In three weeks I had gotten just as far as all the rest had. I could not budge it. Everyone was satisfied that the problem could not be met because the woman had a dominant personality and could not be healed without changing her thinking, without changing certain qualities of her thought. I knew that it would have to be worked out in another way, but in three weeks had accomplished nothing. Then came a telephone call from the woman saying that the pain was terrific and something must be done. In my enthusiasm I said, "I will sit up all night and break this!" My habit then was to do a little reading to find something to give impulse to thought and to meditate, then take a little nap and get up and try again.

At two in the morning the thought came to me, "There is a truth and if I could just lay hold of that truth it would meet this claim. All I need is just one truth and it is hanging around here somewhere! If I just can get it!" Then I went to sleep and in fifteen minutes awakened and heard a voice, "That which I am seeking, I am." I said, "How can that be? I am not the truth." Then I remembered: "Jesus said, 'I am the truth. I am the truth, the way and the light.'[11] And this truth that I am seeking

I am. That makes it very simple, because truth is universal and if I am the truth, this lady is, too. No use sitting up any more."

In the morning the call came in that the case had been met, and there has been no sign to this day of any paralysis. There is no return when we know the truth, when we do not use the truth to overcome an error. When we do, we are acknowledging the power of error and it may come back in double force and surprise us some day because of our own belief that it was a power to begin with and we just got a practitioner to do something about it. From that time on, I have never reached out to try to heal someone out here, or overcome some error, because God is the only power and that is paramount with me. God is the substance and the law of all form.

And remember: the truth itself does nothing for you! It is your consciousness of the truth that makes it work. It is the truth whether you know it or not, but it manifests itself to you only in proportion to your conscious awareness of the truth. In the same way, only the bank account you know about can be of any benefit to you. I myself have gone through a period when some money would have been a welcome thing but I did not know I had it, and then found two accounts in New York City unknown to me for twenty years. There were many times when I would have been very grateful for that money! No, the bank account you do not know you have is no good to you and this truth of the allness of God is of no use to you except in proportion as you can know it and become consciously aware of it.

This is one of the most important things you will ever be called on to realize. Only in proportion as you can see that disease is not a power you do something to, can you meet the appearance called disease, and that is the point I make. There is only one power, one presence. Our good must come through that, not through the human attempt to drag it out of the world from "out here."

One life, one spirit, penetrating all, and that appearance we call death is not death. That appearance we call birth could never be the beginning of life. Life has no beginning and no end and therefore this life which is God is self-maintained and self-sustained, has no opposite and no opposition. Therefore there is no power apart from the one life, which is your life and my life. And that life is eternal. There, too we stand, in this teaching, on the one path—the one life, the one mind.

The treatment, then, lies in the ability to contact this one life—our own soul; one essence, one being which is within our being. In other words, "I live, yet not I; the Christ liveth in me!" The moment we touch the center within our own being, the divine essence of being, we have contacted not only God, but the life of individual man. We have contacted the life of the one calling himself, for the moment, a patient.

It is not necessary for us in our treatment, to send our thought out to a person out there. On the contrary, that is enough to prevent the healing. It is enough to delay the healing, and in some cases makes it impossible. When healing does occur with thought healing, it is because the spiritual consciousness of the patient is so much greater than the ability of that false treatment to stop it.

The correct treatment from the standpoint of spirit or soul, is to go within, and touch the center of one's own being. Never take the name of the patient there. Never take the disease, the claim, whether unemployment, insanity, or disease. Take nothing there but God—and God is already there. Find God! When that little "click" comes—that little sense, that release—when that release comes you will soon get word from the patient that he is healed.

That is my word to you after years and years of practice. Do not take the name or identity or the picture or the thought of your patient into your treatment. Leave these completely outside. You have nothing to do with them. They are illusion to begin with and if you take them into the picture, you do not believe they are illusion but think they are something that you must do something about. It is true, perhaps, that because you have a patient you are fooled for a moment that there is a presence and power apart from God, and so you go within for the illumination, for the light that will dispel the illusion.

Please leave the problem outside! It does not concern you, whether mental, physical, moral or financial. It has nothing to do with you. This treatment is your relationship to God, and when you have become one with God, you have found it. You will feel the release. The presence and power of God will dispel the illusion.

Where do your patients come in? Because they were brought into your consciousness, and inasmuch as the universal consciousness, God, is the mind of the practitioner and also the mind of the patient, there is no transfer of thought from practitioner to patient. There is no need for the transfer of thought, no need for "getting the idea across." Never be guilty of an attempt to give a patient treatment. Study "God, Practitioner and Patient" in *Spiritual Interpretation of Scripture.*

Please remember that God is clearly defined in your thought, that you do not make the mistake of believing that a patient comes to a practitioner, who goes to God, who comes to do the releasing! Or that the patient comes to the practitioner and the practitioner sends something over to the patient. That is all wrong.

God and the practitioner and the patient are really one individual. They are not three and not two. They are just *one*. And the more clearly you recognize that *I Am* is God, and *I Am* is the life and the soul and the mind and the spirit of every individual, the sooner will you realize that we are not dealing with a lot of people but with God infinitely and individually expressed as people—but still God.

When we have that understanding we have the teaching. We are practitioners and we have a teaching to impart. It is not original, but certainly it is true, an individual approach to an age-old truth that God is all.

God literally is all; God constitutes the individual being and body. And now the next question comes up: "What is God?" There is where we have our greatest difficulty because there are several hundred synonyms for the word God, and if you named all of them you would not be any nearer to God. And so we are asking ourselves, "What is God?" Because when we have found God we have found ourselves, and when we have found ourselves, we have found God.

Now it becomes necessary to come down to actual cases and ask ourselves what is God? We all agree on this, that God is the causative principle of the universe. I have said in the *Spiritual Interpretation of Scripture* and in *The Infinite Way*, that God is not a creator. And, of course, I meant that literally, just in the sense that I mean that the principle of mathematics did not create two times two is four. No, it did not create a four and fasten it on to two times two. Two times two includes four, and as soon as two times two came into being, the four was there. God did not put it there, it could not. It was there. It had never been separated from two times two.

In the same way, we cannot say that God created the universe. That would mean there was God and no universe, and then suddenly there was God and a universe. That, somehow, does not make sense to me. But when we think of God as a creative principle, infinite, eternal, omnipresent, without beginning and without ending, then we can see that a cause must be a cause to something and that something we call an "effect." Cause and effect are *one*. Coexistent, co-eternal, and of the same substance.

So we arrive at the truth that God, as creative principle, is the cause of its manifested being appearing as effect. A cause and effect that bind together, like two times two is four, not separate from each other, but always in one place. Wherever the problem is, the answer is, and if the problem is in your thought, the answer is there also. They never get separated from each other—no problem here, and an answer to the problem somewhere else. Always they are one. Now, back to God.

All we know, we know because we are in a state of consciousness. Take away the activity of consciousness and we would have no awareness, no knowledge. We would not know that we existed. In philosophy, Descartes said: "I think, therefore, I am." In the same way we say, "Only because I am conscious, because I am consciousness itself, do I know that I exist, and do I know there is a universe existing." If we can, in a measure, understand ourselves, understand God as consciousness, we can understand this universe as consciousness formed. We can understand this universe, including our body, as a formation of consciousness: incorporeal, spiritual, eternal, coexistent, self-maintained, self-sustained. As two times two is four maintains itself unto eternity, so when we can see that consciousness is the reality of our being, that it is causative principle, then we can say that consciousness becomes evident to us as an infinite variety of forms, and is therefore as eternal as ourselves.

Let us, so far as we can, dwell on the idea, "What Is God," because only in the realization of what God is do we know that which God is God *to*. And that is the effect—or the universe. The importance of that is this: we have taken up, "Seek ye first the kingdom of God (the awareness, the consciousness of God) and his rightness, and all these other things shall be added unto you."[12] Once we have the understanding that our consciousness is the causative principle of our universe, then we know that no matter what we do, this universal consciousness is ever producing and reproducing—just as the law in an orange tree is continuously producing and reproducing oranges.

No matter what we do with the world of effect, the consciousness which is its causative principle, substance and law, is forever producing and reproducing. It is not creating. It is just unfolding, like the moving-picture reel unfolding the entire picture. The picture is already there on the reel; it is only unfolding it to our view.

So with us. We are not depending on yesterday's manna. It makes no difference what becomes of our fortune in assets. It is today that our consciousness is revealing to us its new creation, its new formation. It would make no difference if we lived in a world where we were not permitted to carry possessions over from day to day. Consciousness is always unfolding itself and disclosing itself to us in infinite form, in infinite ways, in infinite varieties. We are never dependent. No regrets over our past lives, no regrets over what we have lost in the past. It has nothing to do with today. Today our consciousness is unfolding and disclosing itself in every new way, in every new form, and always increasing abundantly.

This subject of God is an infinite one. We will come back to it over and over again, because it is the next most important part of our work. Without the knowledge of God, we would have no knowledge of the effect of God, which is our universe.

I want to teach on living this Christ. In the Bible we have certain laws. We have known them mostly as quotations, without taking them seriously as something to be lived. But one of the greatest laws of the Bible is the law of forgiveness, of praying for one's enemies. You may take that very seriously, because it is a proven law.

The idea of forgiveness does not mean looking at a human being and remembering the terrible offense he committed against us and then forgiving him for it. There is no virtue in that. The virtue lies in the ability to see through the human to the divinity of his being, realizing that in the divinity of his being there has never been an occasion for error of any nature. It is as if he were asking us for help and we would have to behold him as he really is–a spiritual being.

Without their asking for help, we are called on every day to look upon those toward whom we have any negative feeling, and develop this act of forgiveness, which means to turn to the Christ of our own being and there know that nothing but love exists. There never has been a mortal and all that appears as a mortal is the Christ itself, incorrectly seen.

That ability to forgive is one of the greatest laws of the Bible. Praying for our enemies is the same idea. It does not mean we are to believe that the other fellow can shoot us first; it means the ability to understand God as the life and the mind of individual man, and to know there is no other mind but that one. Appearances have nothing to do with it at all. We are dealing with the reality of being.

In *Spiritual Interpretation of Scripture* we have this unfoldment: that the characters of the Bible are the qualities of our own thought. Every character in the Bible really exists now in your thought and in mine. We have them all there. For instance, we think of Moses and wonder just what part he plays. You will remember that Moses led the Hebrews out of their religious and economic darkness, into a more abundant sense of human life, into a greater sense of religious freedom, into greater territorial expansion. Therefore, Moses must represent a higher type of humanhood.

When first we turned to metaphysical truth, the chances are that in almost every case the purpose for it was to find just that: a greater sense of religious freedom or economic freedom or physical freedom in the sense of health—and our first demonstrations were just along those lines. They consisted of improved humanhood, they were not really the Christ at all. We used the language and thought we were demonstrating the Christ, but we were not in most cases really receiving the spiritual vision. We went from twenty to thirty dollars a week or from a sick heart to a healthy heart, or from a sick lung to a healthy lung. We increased the degree of freedom in our human experience.

There was, then, that quality in our thought which led us to a metaphysical truth and ultimately led us to a greater sense of freedom in our human experience. And so Moses is the quality of thought that will lead one out of the darkness of human experience into greater human freedom and good. That thought must have been in consciousness, or no one would have been led out.

Now, what is the Jesus quality or thought in our consciousness? It is that which is to lead us out of our human good, into spiritual good. It is that which is to lead us out of humanhood with a little more income or health, into the realization of our spiritual self-hood. Therefore, we have the Savior, or Christ, within our own consciousness.

The mind that was in Christ Jesus is the mind of us. Remember that Jesus told us this: "Before Abraham was I am."[13] And he also said, "Lo, I am with you unto the end of the world."[14] He was not speaking of his humanhood, because it was not here before Abraham and is not here today. But the I that he spoke of—which was the Christ—was in human consciousness before Abraham and is in our consciousness this minute.

So the very quality we would call Jesus, which is the presence of the Christ (or healing, or the saving Christ), is the quality of our consciousness this moment. And when we realize it now, we should be very well satisfied that the Christ is the healing consciousness, is part of our human consciousness, and is operating while we are sleeping. It really is a healing influence; it is really and truly what the Aramaic language knew as Messiah; what the Greeks knew as Savior; what we know as the Christ or Savior. That is not a man of two thousand years ago, but a quality of our own consciousness this very moment.

All the way through the Bible we can find that each character of the Bible is represented in our consciousness as some quality or activity. For that reason I always recommend that students in this work refer to the Unity Metaphysical Dictionary. It is the finest on the market today and it gives all the spiritual interpretations of characters and places and events and rivers of the Bible. This work was begun by Swedenborg. He was the first to bring forth a spiritual interpretation of Scripture that is called *Genesis and Apocalypse* and in it he defines, spiritually, certain rivers and characters appearing in the Bible. But that was only the beginning. The work was then carried on by Unity in Kansas City and many of their students, over a long period of years, finally produced what is now that dictionary. In it you will find how true it is that you have every one of those characters in your consciousness.

In *Spiritual Interpretation of Scripture* I have shown how Joseph has every quality of the brethren in his own being and he had to meet them and overcome them. You will always find it helpful to turn to that book in order to work out some of the problems through the realization that these are qualities within our own being, to realize that such qualities are helpful in their turn but may be harmful if we do not reverse them and realize them in their true light.

It was quite a revelation to me when I realized this–that this experience of Joseph, which had been brought on by his brothers, was not really error, but God itself driving Joseph into Egypt where he could fulfill his missions. If you could have heard some of the things I have heard from people about the beliefs of error that brought them into the realization of that which it was necessary for them to know, you would better understand Joseph.

In our realization, then—and I am bringing in this point again only to show that God in its infinity is your individual consciousness—it is our consciousness that contains the entire universe. It is our consciousness that becomes the law unto our world; and this very moment that we can consciously feel and realize the presence of the Christ, we have that quality of being which to our sense annihilates every form and belief of sin or erroneous condition in our experience.

For home reading will you begin with "Unveiling the Christ," "Grace," and "Cleansing the Temple," in *Spiritual Interpretation of Scripture.*

It is inevitable that as we go out from here, having been together ("Where two or more are gathered in my name. . ."[15]), that we go out with a higher consciousness than that with which we came in. Then when we read, we are more apt to be able to discern spiritually, the intent of the words we are reading. Ordinarily, we just read print and occasionally we catch a spiritual glimpse, but the higher we are in spiritual consciousness, the easier it is spiritually to discern what we read. So it is important to be lifted up into a higher consciousness and from there do our reading and thinking. In that way these higher revelations can unfold to us.

Do not memorize these words thinking they will do anything for you. You cannot meet a problem on the level of the problem. The problem comes to us as sin, disease, lack, limitation, death, unemployment, homelessness, and so forth. The moment we start to do anything about it on that level, we are unable to meet it. Therefore, when a problem is presented to you, drop it

and turn within until you attain that center of consciousness where you feel the release and the whole problem
has disappeared. If you work on the problem, if you start
to work to achieve something, that moment you have
defeated your purpose.

How are we to accomplish this finding the center of
our being? First of all, turn away from the problem.
Forget it and close your eyes and take some quotation
into your thought, preferably a very short one like, "I
and the Father are one" or "Be still and know that I am
God."[16] As you think on that quotation and your thought
starts to wander back and forth, and perhaps you wonder what to have for luncheon and so on, pay no attention to these thoughts. Let them come and let them go;
it does no harm for them to come and go. You keep your
attention on, "I and the Father are one" or on any
suitable short quotation from Scripture or metaphysical
writings. As you lose the thread, just gently come back to
it and say, "I wandered off, but 'I and the Father are
one.'" Bring your attention back again and again. As
many times as you lose the thread, just gently bring it
back. This is not a mental process, there is no hurry
about it. Just gently come back to, "I and the Father are
one."

After you have done this for two to five minutes, you
will find yourself getting a little more at peace. If it is
possible then, in that moment of quietness, remember
that you are listening for the "still small voice."[17] Remember to keep your ear open as if there were a message just outside waiting to come in.

You are now developing a state of receptivity to the
still small voice. So, as you hold it here gently, "I and the
Father are one, I and the Father are one," all the time the

ear is listening. A sense of peace is settling down on you. When your release comes, when that sense of peace comes, the problem has been met, either your own or someone else's, or you come right down to the realization. That is when you begin to feel this divine intelligence.

~ 3 ~

STATES AND STAGES OF CONSCIOUSNESS

THE READING ASSIGNMENT TONIGHT will begin in "States and Stages of Consciousness" in *Spiritual Interpretation of Scripture,* and continue to the end of the book. The reason for this assignment is this: I want to tell you tonight that the mental and the spiritual are not synonymous. In the metaphysical world, it has been believed for many years, that mental and spiritual healing are the same thing, whereas they are actually as far apart as material and spiritual healing.

What is mental healing? Mental and material healing are the same thing on two levels of consciousness. The mental is a little higher and lighter than the material. But they are two strata of the same belief. You have heard the terms "mentally spiritual" or "spiritually mental." That is exactly the same as saying "a godly devil." They are that far apart, not that one is necessarily right and one is wrong. They are different levels of consciousness and they are as far apart as the North and South Poles.

The reason for this mixture of the spiritual and the mental goes back to the beginning of mental practice. Mental practice was originated in Germany by Franz Anton Mesmer, the physician who discovered animal magnetism. He discovered that there is an invisible vital fluid, a mental fluid that passes through the practitioner and the patient and that it acts hypnotically through suggestion. One of Mesmer's students came to New England, landed in Portland, Maine, and found a student there named Quimby. Mesmer's student taught this mesmerism, then known as hypnotism or animal magnetism, to Mr. Quimby and for many years they engaged in this activity for entertainment purposes.

Mr. Quimby later became known as Dr. Quimby, and came to have with him a young patient, or student, who worked as assistant. This boy developed the faculty, under hypnotism, of discerning the mental cause for the physical diseases of people coming on the platform. He passed this on to Mr. Quimby who, by recognizing the non-power of the mental thought, erased the disease. He began to have wonderful healings. He then gave up the entertainment work and became a very well-known healer with people coming from all over the country, and there are reports of amazing healings.

Dr. Quimby was a very good and religious man in a church sense, and very soon he started to bring terms like "God" or "the Christ" into the terminology of his work. As a matter of fact, I believe it was Quimby who first made the distinction between Jesus and Christ, understanding Jesus to be the man and Christ the spirit that animated him. Up to that time, in the theological world, Jesus Christ was supposed to be one. In metaphysical language now, we understand Jesus to be the man and Christ to be the power or presence or spirit of God which animated him. And so in that way, religious terms entered into the mental practice.

Mrs. Eddy was Dr. Quimby's best known student. She traveled for three years, lecturing for Dr. Quimby on the

Science of Quimbyism which he later called the Science of Christ or Christian Science. Mrs. Eddy, as you all know, had a very religious background, well steeped in the Bible and well steeped in religious thought, and she too brought all the religious terms into the mental practice.

Now, let us not deceive ourselves. It *was* a mental practice. It was so mental that when she was out in the healing work she very often had to send a letter to Quimby to "please rescue her, she had taken on the disease of the patient she was healing." Those early letters will show that it was a mental practice even though they were using such terms as "the Christ." It was one mind over another mind, or mind over matter, or one mind understanding that disease was not a power. It was primarily suggestion, the transfer of the thoughts of one mind to another.

As time went on, other students came into the work through other avenues as well. Mr. Dresser started the New Thought Movement and the Fillmores started Unity. The Unity Movement was begun in 1892, two years before the original Mother Church in Boston was built. They all came in at about this time. And while it is true that some of the students and practitioners adhered closely to the mental, others, who were of a spiritual disposition, advanced in the spiritual field.

We have come to that place in metaphysical work where we have two distinct branches. Very few people will acknowledge it, but it is true; we have the mental and the spiritual. If you were to search the New Testament you would find no authority for most of what is now mental practice, although that mental practice still utilizes the name and nature of the Christ. It is that fact I want to bring forth tonight.

The human mind is not a power. Of course, the human mind is a power on the level of the human mind, and that is why a good strong human mind can overcome a weak one. When I use the word power, I mean it in its absolute, true sense, and the human mind is not a power in that sense. It will not enable one person to injure another person mentally. Also, any good that you are deriving from the activity of the human mind is a temporal, finite good, and must never be confused with the activity of that mind which was in Christ Jesus.

Our basis, then, insofar as metaphysical work is concerned, is that the human mind is not the power in spiritual healing. In the New Testament, if you will follow the teachings of Jesus Christ, you will find these quotations: "Take no thought for your life, what ye shall eat and what ye shall drink or wherewithal ye shall be clothed."[1] Now, take our mental practitioners where they ask the patient, "Do you want a demonstration of supply, a house or an automobile?" Or, the patient may ask the practitioner to "demonstrate" a room to live in, or a husband, or to demonstrate getting rid of one. You know that is true! There is not a practitioner of any experience who has not had, at times, the very sad experience, the very pitiful one, of having people come and ask for a home, an automobile, a husband or a wife. Yes, every kind of demonstration in the world, including black magic!

Here is the point: even on the highest level of that type of practice, it is against the teaching of the Christ! The Christ says to take *no* thought for your life, or for your supply, or for your clothing. It goes on and gives you the whole list of what not to ask for, tells you why, and ends up in this wonderful way: "Your heavenly

Father knoweth what things ye have need of, and it is his good pleasure to give you the kingdom!"[2] Therefore, to try to go to God with some finite problem would be against the teachings of the Christ. Further, "Who, by taking thought, can add one cubit to his stature?"[3] Did you ever think about that?

When you are sitting down to take thought of adding something to your supply or your health, you will fail. "Who, by taking thought? . . ." Again, the Bible tells us: "My thoughts are not your thoughts, my ways are not your ways."[4] Yet here we are believing that if we will just do some right thinking, hold the right thought, just send out the right thought, it will do something for us! And all the time we are working against the very teaching that we claim to be following, when we quote, "Take no thought for your life, take no thought for what you shall eat."

There is a saying, "Thoughts are things," and there you have the very proof of what I am saying. Thoughts *are* things. Thoughts are on the level of things—just two different strata of the same belief, one a little more coarse than the other. But, thoughts *are* things! It is only when you get away from thought that you get away from things and come into the realm of idea, and idea is not a thing. Idea is an activity and a quality of mind, but of the divine mind and not of the human mind.

The transfer of thought from one individual to another is the activity of the human mind. Although it often results in what we call a healing or improving, it is, at best, merely temporary. It is a temporary improvement, for the reason that if you succeed today, you must work twice as hard next week, and the end of all this mental practice is headache! These people who become adept in mental work begin tightening up, work under pressure, and it is mental pressure. Those who work without this active thought-taking process, become relaxed. They become, instead of themselves being a force or power, merely the vehicle through which the spirit works. They are never disappointed, never irritable, never get off on tangents. There is no reason for it, because the spirit is ever renewing, ever re-building. The spirit is doing that, not my taking thought.

Probably some of you, when giving mental treatments, have seen the reaction on those who received the treatment. Some of you have watched practitioners (and perhaps yourselves), who have studied all this terrific mental pressure business, and have seen the confusion it brought and have not even known what did it.

For sixteen years I was in the Science practice and it was just as rife there as it was on the outside; there was just as much authority in Mrs. Eddy's writings for mental practice as for spiritual practice. Both are shown forth in her writings and you can take your choice, whichever one suits you best. I personally never made any headway with the mental practice and could not indulge in it, but I have seen results from those who have used it, and have seen the results on those who have permitted themselves to come under the mental treatment of another person "holding thoughts" for them, dominating them, almost at times controlling them.

Another thing in connection with this spiritual healing: Under the dominion of the Spirit, under the dominion of the mind that was in Christ Jesus, it would be absolutely impossible to violate your own spiritual integrity. You could not possibly cheat or defraud or overcharge a patient or be unfaithful in your duty to a patient; the spirit would not let you, would not give you a thought or impulse in that direction. Yet when under the mental influence, you have your choice of being good or bad, with no controlling power to prevent your doing what you want to do, except your own highest sense of right.

That does not mean that those working along mental lines are necessarily bad or wrong. I bring this out only to show that if they are good, they are so because they are good persons, not because they have come under the influence of "that mind which was in Christ Jesus," which permits them to be nothing less than God in action. That is what I mean.

Another thing—when an individual comes under the dominion of that mind which was also in Christ Jesus, they heal without mental or personal effort, whether the patient is awake or asleep, and even when the practitioner is asleep! I am going to ask you a question: How many of you have ever been in an office with me for an oral or a silent treatment and have gone out without feeling some beneficial effect? Some feeling, some influence, some peace? How very many have told me they felt that sense of peace! All right, now I want to ask you: How many believe it is necessary to be in an office or a room with me to get that reaction? How many believe that my body or my brain has anything to do with it?

No! you could sit in your home in China and receive the same divine impulse from any individual in whom the mind of Christ is even in a tiny measure apparent, and I do not myself claim more than a grain of it. But that one grain does miracles when left to operate without mental manipulation, with the mental desire to reach out to the consciousness or the mind or thought of the individual seeking help.

How many times have you heard someone call up and be sure they had arthritis or cancer or consumption, and then realize it "just could not have been," they were healed so fast! The chances are it was not there. But the point is, suppose you accept the diagnosis presented to you and sit down to work on it? Nine times out of ten you would be working on the wrong thing. And if they brought you a doctor's diagnosis, it could still be fifty-five percent wrong. In medical returns from Massachusetts General Hospital one year, you will find that their own check-up of diagnoses in their own hospital for that year was but forty-five per cent correct, even with x-rays, blood tests and urinalyses!

Supposing you were to accept such a diagnosis and go to work. You would be up in a tree. No! If you had a medical diagnosis you would be only partly correct, and without it (just taking your patient's word) you are bound to be seventy-five to ninety percent wrong. So what good is your treatment if you have given it for a specific claim? If they get well, they must have done so in spite of your treatment!

As a matter of fact, since disease is an unreality, since it is a belief that really cannot be localized, all of this mental handling is nonsense. Illusion! In my entire life I have never met an individual with enough hate in his system to cause anything as rotten as cancer, not one so bad as that, and I don't think you have. There must be a different reason for it. In the same way you have heard that consumption and tuberculosis are caused by lust. A person that would have that much lust would be locked up in an institution. No—people just are not that bad.

And now for the books! I read an article last year about a woman with flat feet. She had her thought analyzed by a practitioner and it turned out her son was killed in the war and she grieved so much she lost her understanding and got flat feet. Again, a woman had athlete's foot and could not be healed, and her practitioner had examined her thought and discovered she had a desire for human affection! My comment at that time was, "Practitioners are going to be busy with only athlete's foot. With so much affection in the world, none of us should do too badly!" That is what all this mental cause for physical effect comes down to. Mrs. Eddy once gave out a list of mental causes for physical diseases and after about a year recalled them all.

If there ever was a time when health came through handling those mental causes, take my word for it, they were belief healings; a belief of disease healed by entertaining a belief of a cause and a cure—one belief acting upon another belief. I have read the New Testament until I have worn out the book and I cannot find Jesus once saying anything about affection causing a disease. He said, instead, that "even sin had not caused a man to be blind."[5]

Now, let us get this straightened out, because in so much metaphysical literature you have these opposites. I do not know literature well enough to quote it although I have read much, but I do know Mrs. Eddy's writings well enough to quote them and you will find samples like this: "The procuring cause and foundation of all disease is ignorance, sin and fear." And eight pages later: "Neither disease itself, sin, nor fear, has the power to cause disease or relapse." And, "Immortal Mind is the only cause, therefore disease is neither cause nor effect." And again, "Mortal mind produces disease and Immortal Mind cures it." Those are samples.

Now you who are here are here only because, "my
sheep hear my voice,"[6] because we are on the level of
consciousness where we are finished if we ever did work
in that mental realm. We must come into the place now
where we choose to work in accordance with the principles laid down in the Science of Christ, which is a
revelation or teaching of Christ Jesus and, of course, we
know what the answer is. We have one of the greatest
quotations in all the world on that subject: "Not by
might, nor by power, but by my spirit."[7] There is no
better way to heal than that, a way that will leave your
patient freer to function as the normal presentation of
God, without undue influence of other humans. "Not by
might, nor by power, but by my spirit." By my spirit, the
spirit of God, that mind which was also in Christ–the
mind of you and the mind of me.

The mind that was in Christ Jesus is as available to
you today as if Jesus were sitting in this room. Otherwise
you would have to say, "Oh, no, I will have to see the
body." That is not true. If you do not believe it, try this
experiment: Some time when you are feeling tired or ill
and you have the opportunity to be off by yourself, just
close your eyes and ask yourself whether the mind that
was in Christ Jesus was inside his brain or inside his
body, or did he tell the truth when he said, "Before
Abraham was I am."[8] and "Lo, I will be with you unto
the end of the world,"[9] and "If I go not away, the
Comforter will not come unto you."[10]

If you believe those words to be true, just sit back and
say, "All right, mind of Christ Jesus, Father within, the
Christ–as long as you are with me, I can sit back and
rest in peace!" And then settle back and rest in peace.
See if you won't have an instantaneous healing without

taking thought. At first you may not be healed of your more serious claims and problems because we are still in that place where we might not be able to accept that healing without thinking we had seen a miracle. When you are tired and wondering, rest back for two minutes in the mind that was in Christ Jesus, and see if it is not as available to you here and now as if Jesus were in the room.

I know it is true, because for so many years I have encouraged my friends and patients to reach out to my consciousness, regardless of where I was. You are not going to reach out to Joel Goldsmith, but to the mind that was in Christ Jesus. I am never going to limit you to my human mind. My one mind is the realization that the mind of Christ Jesus is the mind of me, available to all, whether I am close or far. That is the secret of living in the Christ-consciousness, the secret of my work. Paul's statement, "I live, yet not I, Christ liveth in me"[11] is true; every time anyone reaches out to me, he is reaching the Christ, which is really living as me.

I said to you this afternoon, "Be grateful that every truth that is a truth is a universal truth, not only about Jesus Christ, but about everyone in the world who will open his consciousness and accept it." Accept it, not about a human being, because a human being is limited to his human, educated mind of experience, personality and birth, but accept it about any individual who will open his consciousness and say, "Yes, anything that was true of Jesus, Moses, Elijah, Elisha or Paul or John, is true of me. Otherwise it could not be a truth, but only a personal sense."

Therefore, if you want that mind that was in Christ Jesus continuously, open your consciousness. That brings us to the point of why we need not exercise mental power, why we do not have to direct our thought to a certain part of the body or a certain cause for the disease or to any person.

What were the causes for all the lack and limitation during the depression? Why should those not to blame for it have been paying the penalty? The first discovery that I made in my practice the first year was this: error is not in any individual's thinking! This shocked me, because I had always been taught that one is a wrong thinker. I discovered in that first year this is not true. A baby does not suffer because his parents hate it or are thinking wrong, but from universal beliefs which his parents do not know how to handle and overcome. You do not get colds, flu and polio in their seasons because of your wrong thinking: There is a universal belief and you don't know how to meet and overcome it.

Our weakness in metaphysical practice is that we love to tell how wonderful God is, and we hate to tell the other fellow what to do about the appearance of sin and disease. If you cling to this "God is love" business without learning how to handle it, you will be as badly off as if you did not discover that God is love! Would there be a single person experiencing lust, animality, fear or false appetite, if he knew how to handle it? There is a law of God that annuls these. You must know it, and just saying God is love does not do it, because we already have too much of that in the world—even among people who are sure that God is love.

Do not forget that every evil circumstance in your life can be prevented. Nobody is a victim of anything but his ignorance of the laws of life. God never intended we should know old age or any of these other horrors we are seeing. God never intended that we have cripples or drunkards or dope fiends, and there is no reason in the world why we do, except that we have never learned how to destroy our human belief about them. They do not exist as God created things. He does not punish us with them, or with that old Hebrew law, "The sins of the father shall be visited unto the children."[12] And you know, even the Hebrews saw how terrible this law was and rescinded it two hundred years later: "No more shall it be said in Israel that the parents have eaten sour grapes and the children's teeth are set on edge."[13] Even they, in the ignorance of those dark ages, learned in just two hundred years not to blame God for the horrible thing such as punishing of children. Yes, the Hebrews learned that three or four thousand years ago, and we should be at least that far advanced.

Today we still have laws of heredity, and all the ills of the father visited on the children, grandchildren and great-grandchildren. We must rise higher than that. We can make a beginning by understanding that there is a law of God in operation in individual and collective being, in us as individuals, in us as groups, races and nations.

There is a law of God, but we have got to begin to bring that law into operation by giving up our egotistical beliefs that any kind of thinking we can do is a power or that taking a statement and drilling it in will finally make it come true. Maybe it will come true, but it is hard work and it is not permanent and not spiritual and it leaves something missing in the mentality; first, because it permits others to dominate our thoughts, and then because it takes away from us our realization of the only one real power there is, which is God, whose kingdom is within us. The kingdom of God is within us.

Reciting that two times two is four won't make it so, though it might help us to remember that it is so. An affirmation, repeated in thought, will help to impress us with the truth that is true, but in doing so, we really give up a good deal of freedom. It would be far better to hear a truth, or read a truth, and let the truth do the work, since Jesus said, "I am the truth,"[14] and truth is a synonym for God. Why let your manipulation of truth be the agency for healing? Why not let truth do it alone? Do you see the difference, the reliance you will build up, in the confidence that there is truth?

How many really and truly believe there is a God? We accept it and talk about it, but how many cling to a medicine and to a thought, and really, neither the medicine nor the thought can ever be God. God is not thought; thought is not God power. Thought is an avenue of awareness. Thought is not power, but thought is an avenue of awareness. You can memorize that statement, not to make it come true, but when you are attempting to manipulate thoughts remembering that may give you a good laugh! *Thought is not power.*

~ 4 ~

THOUGHT IS NOT POWER

IT POPPED INTO MY HEAD ONE DAY that thought is not a power, it is an avenue of awareness. It shocked me for a moment, having it come out of a clear sky when I was not asking for it. Then I saw that I, through the avenue of thought, can become aware of people in this room and know whether they are dressed in brown or green or black, but no amount of thinking I do can make it so. Not my thought and not all the thought in this room will change that which is in this room. Therefore, thought, to me, becomes an avenue of awareness.

Through thought I have become aware of the great truth that you are the Christ of God. That is what you are and have been since time began. It just took me a long time to find it out–and others are still finding it out. But it was always true, since, "Before Abraham was I am," and nobody's thinking did it. It just is so, as a law of God; and, "Lo, I will be with you always . . ."[1] even unto the end of this human belief of things. Certainly I will, and that is the Christ, the mind that was in Christ Jesus, the soul or spirit of God.

If we took all the practitioners out of business today, it should make no difference to a person who has been on this path for any length of time. Our great sin is when

59

we have patients or students for a year or two who still have not learned that God is their infinite, individual, invisible, eternal life, when we have not made it sufficiently clear that the body is the temple of the living God. With a year of this kind of instruction, a body should be reflecting it.

The minute you begin to know that the mind that was in Christ Jesus is your mind, from that moment on it is doing something to your body, your business, your income, your human relationships and family relationships. It may seem slow in the beginning, unless you have a tremendous light such as Saul had when he became Paul. In that case it might be quick, but even there, it was nine years after Saul had that experience before he went out on a mission tour. It took that long to digest, unfold and come forth. So with us.

Sometimes we catch a tremendous light of truth. I noticed this in the days I was sending out my weekly letter. Only two years later, on rereading them, would I understand certain statements and feel an inner conviction or realization of them. I knew it was true when I wrote it, but many were the statements which only two or three years later registered with me, and I said, "That was right!" And so with us.

You will be voicing many, many truths today which you intellectually agree are truths, but which you will not realize and which will really register only one or two years from now. That is because it takes all that time to come down from the level of our egotistical sense and really register in consciousness. If we were all really lifted up in spiritual consciousness, what I have said tonight here would lift all of us into heaven—but one statement is registered with an individual here and one with another there, and many have not registered with me. They are coming through from the spirit, but it takes a degree of spiritual awareness to be able to digest and catch them. I am sure many statements I make tonight will startle me when I hear them again. I have often said, "Where did I ever get that?" It had not yet registered.

One such statement is from Jesus: "My kingdom is not of this world."[2] I don't know how that registered with you but I can tell you that for the last five years at least, that quotation has been my life and my blood and my bones—and all that goes to make up me. "My kingdom is not of this world." After having been told that my kingdom is not of this world, what do you think of me when I start in doing some mental work for next month's rent? If it is not part of this world, I don't know what it is! What would you think of a person who, being told that the Christly kingdom has nothing to do with this world, went around worrying whether he was married or single? This point should be very clear to you. Don't die and go to another world, but right here where we are, is that world visible to us only through our spiritual sense.

We are always *in* the world in the sense of having everything that everyone else has and having it a little better, but not *of* it in the sense that we have any concern for it. We let it unfold and become a part of our being.

To illustrate: We are in San Francisco and at this minute, within one square mile, there is every kind of entertainment and amusement that the human mind can think of, on low as well as on high levels. Yet we are here. And I wonder—and you can prove it by asking a few thousand people—if there is anything more dull and uninteresting than a metaphysical lecture, if anything would bore them more than this! I know thousands of people who would pay good money to be able to stay away from this, and hundreds of people who could not be dragged here to please anyone!

Why do we sort of like it? (And we do!) Because we are already in a different world than they are in, and we do not have to die to get there. We have different friends than they have. One spiritual quotation, one spiritual thought, gives us more joy than the finest movie playing in town. Why? Because we are no longer in that world where that is the measure of our joy. We have left that world without having to die or become ridiculous, like stopping eating or giving up the wearing of clothes—nothing of an abnormal nature. Yet we left that world. How many of those twenty-five cent thrillers and crime novels were sold in San Francisco today? Yet look at us. Instead of paying a quarter for that, we pay twenty-five dollars for this! What is wrong with us? We are in a different world; we left that other world.

Another thing: You know there are loads of people who actually believe they can not make a good, honest living without doing a little chiseling or cheating or something. You know as well as I do how many business people today believe you can only get by with political influence or this or that. Yet, here we are, a group of people who have learned, at least, that there is a principle at work within us that enables us to live completely in accord with the law of Christ Jesus, with the laws laid down in the Golden Rule; that we actually can adopt a principle like that for ourselves and be abundantly fed—and I mean abundantly—if we want to make the effort to claim it.

That is what I mean by living in a different world. Most could never agree that you do not have to use human ingenuity, physical force, or mental pressure, and we know that these are not necessary. We can go along and be normal, harmonious, spiritual, and yet attract to us all that is part of our demonstration. How? (Not that any of us now are going to think of this as an affirmation . . .) "My oneness with God constitutes my oneness with every spiritual idea. That spiritual idea will express itself as a home, a friend, a student, a patient, book or teacher—anything of which I have need!" My oneness with God! I do not go out demonstrating those things. I demonstrate only my oneness with God by opening my consciousness to that truth, accepting it and letting it become part of my consciousness. Then that truth does the work.

So we come to this point: What is the motive for our study? Because on that depends all of our future in this work. I do not mean that those of you who cannot grasp what I am saying may not go back to the mental again. If necessary, that is what you will have to do until you are able to come up out of it. But to those who have caught the glimpse of this, the whole of your future is going to depend on whether or not you can determine to seek only the consciousness of the presence of God, and let the things be added. That is going to be the measure of your demonstration.

The moment that we start taking thought for anything in the world that can be seen, heard, tasted, touched or smelled, we are taking thought for this world, and Jesus said, "My kingdom is not of this world." And it is not. You may, in thinking of your own existence, start to do some mental work for place, business, companionship, marriage—all the time having in your mind San Francisco as the locale. Yet, right at this very moment your demonstration may be Africa, and you have closed your

whole mind to it because you never even thought about
that. Africa did not enter your thought at all!

However, if instead of taking thought for anything
that had to do with person, place or thing, your entire
work had been for the conscious realization of the mind
that was also in Christ Jesus, you would have heard it
voiced or received a letter telling you that something
was waiting for you in Africa, or China, or somewhere
else. In other words, it is sinful to limit. It is sinful to put
any kind of mental limitation on our demonstrations.
How do you know where it is going to be, when or with
whom, if there is God governing its own universe?
Where do you or I have the nerve to come in and limit
or even outline that demonstration?

We have no right to outline. Only to abide in principles. One of those is, "Take no thought for your life."[3] I
hear the telephone bell ring. A voice says, "Work for life,
I am dying." The Bible says, "Take no thought for life!"
So I say, "Yes Ma'am, I will work for God." Life is a
synonym for God. Since God is the only life, can you see
what happens to any mental work for life? It comes back
and hits you with death, and you say, "All that I was
doing was thinking about the absence of life, and I got it!"

A practitioner once said to a patient, "There is no life
in your body!" But the patient wanted it more abundantly, and wanted to manifest it—if not in, then certainly
as a body. Again, how many of us are trying to get rid of
our bodies, denying the body? Can you picture what we
would look like without bodies? No! Don't try to demonstrate without a body! Don't deny money. Don't deny a
home. But don't take thought for them. Let them come in
the form that God has outlined for you. That is the only
difference.

Don't deny the body. You have a body and God gave it to you, not your parents. Not any one of you who is a parent knows enough to make a body. No, you have all you can do to stand still for nine months! God formed your body, parents didn't. I once said to a mother, "At best you were the oven in which your child was baked!"

God is spirit and expresses itself infinitely and individually and has its own way of producing its image and likeness. This that we see is only our concept of an already divine activity. Human parentage—human creation—is not spiritual, is not of God. If it were, everyone would be harmonious and normal and there would be no discordant or deformed children. It is only because we have left God out of it that we have those conditions.

Do not fool yourself that we are not responsible for these troubles. We look at human birth as if it were just an animalistic thing. It is not. That is a false interpretation. It in itself is divine and wonderful. We turn it into something of an animal nature. We must learn to reinterpret it. And what will happen when we do? We won't have so many divorces. The only reason for divorce is that we see each other as man and woman. It is a hard thing for a man and a woman to live together for many years and not get fed up with each other. If, long before marriage, we get the idea that we are not seeking marriage or home or companionship but are seeking the presence of God in visible form, then you would be surprised at the marriages and birthrate we would have. Every child would be God made manifest. There would be no material creation.

Back again to what is our motive in this study. Is it merely to change sickness into health, lonesomeness into companionship, homelessness into a home? Or are we ready, at this moment, to stop taking thought for the things of this world which do not belong to the spiritual kingdom and merely say, "I can truthfully say that all I want is the kingdom of God on earth. That is all I want. What I want is the kingdom of God on earth—the reign of God in my individual experience, the government of God in my individual affairs."

Now, the minute we say that, we are seeking the kingdom of God and his rightness. Those of you who heard me Sunday will remember that that was the entire point. What we are to seek is not our sense of right-ness—more dollars, more companionship, more health. We are to seek his rightness—the spiritual sense of good. If you knew the spiritual sense of supply, you would find it to be far different from our present sense. The spiritual sense of health would be much different from our standard, which sets a normal span of sixty or seventy years. But his rightness, his standard of health, would be one that would enable us to live on earth as long as we desired, as long as we did not get lonesome for those who had gone on before us.

There are people on earth today two hundred years of age, and I know of one man about whom there is authority for knowing he is over six hundred years of age with no desire to find another world. That is possible if you can agree that it is not the physical sense of health or life you are desiring—not merely longevity. It is the spiritual sense of God, health, immortality.

What is immortality? It is not living a long time. Immortality is actual life eternal without ending, with the actual realization that it never began. You only begin to understand time when you can begin to have a little memory of what happened before 1900. Nobody here ever expects to have an end to his consciousness, even though you all might believe that it is inevitable that you will drop your body. You can correct that thought right now. You don't have to drop it or permit it to age unless you want to. But you must make the conscious decision that life is eternal and your body, the temple of the living God, is under the jurisdiction of that life.

Since life is eternal and life is consciousness, why should consciousness be dead or dead to the past? Through your own consciousness of being–not through memory–you have existed eternally, and you will exist eternally, with this difference: that in your inner enlightenment you can go on existing without that transfer, that moment of passing, which the world calls "death" but which is only transition. Then why have it, when you can make the transition as you have now, out of that world of mortal beliefs into this world of spiritual reality? You can just as well make the transition from this world into the one where you live without taking thought.

Let no one believe that all I have said about not taking thought has anything to do with becoming a mental blank. On the contrary–the moment you learn to live without taking thought, you will be the most mentally active person in the community, because that is when you are not animated by your own limited sense of mind. The mind that was in Christ Jesus starts functioning as you. If you want to write, you will be a writer; if you want to paint, you will be a painter, because there will be no more limitation. You do not become a mental blank, and you do not live in a vacuum, but your thought is so animated by this spiritual mind that you are thinking even when you are sleeping. You are not taking thought. That is quite a different thing. You are receiving divine impulses which we call thought, or avenues of awareness, and you really become aware in infinitely bigger versions of experience.

Let us never believe that living without taking thought compels any kind of laziness. It brings such activity of life, the wonder is that we ever get to sleep. There is no end to the activity that comes to the person whose being is animated with the spiritual or Christ mind. You are bringing forth the most marvelous thoughts, which are the thoughts of God—God's thoughts pouring out as man—instead of digging around in your brain for some used up thoughts, cold truths. And what truth is a cold truth? A cold truth is something you remember as a quotation. When a thought comes to your open consciousness it comes as a hot truth, a live truth, and it carries out the healing and brings with it inventiveness and new ideas. That is what it is when we receive a direct impartation from the divine mind.

You can go digging around all of the old books for ages back (and these cold truths really go back a long way) but they do not do us any good until they come to us, to our open consciousness. Therefore, the biggest part of this teaching is not imparting knowledge or giving you statements of truth, because every statement I give you now, you have known long ago. But the real value of this teaching is to develop in you a state of spiritual receptivity, so that you can be as receptive to the Christ mind as I am. That is what this teaching is for—not to build me up or to create a following. Neither is it concerned primarily or mentally with seeing whether you have a healthy or sick body, although bringing out health is a great part of this work.

The main idea I am trying to convey is receptivity to the Christ. Open your consciousness, so that you will receive all of these truths. Open your consciousness to the inflow of the Christ, so that your open consciousness becomes the living Christ, becomes the light of the world.

That is our teaching today. Many people think there is going to be another Coming soon but I think you are and I am that coming. Every one of us is now coming into that age when we can accept Jesus' statement that the Comforter will come to us when we stop relying on human people and modes and means; when we can open up our consciousness to the whole infinite Christ, then Christ, the Second Coming, will come to you and to me. I cannot believe, though, for a minute, that any Second Coming is coming to the fellow who has no time to learn to know the Christ.

We must experience the Christ, not by hearsay but by actual demonstration, by actual contact. Only a few of you know that it is possible. I myself have seen that in working with those of receptive thought I can lift them to where they can see the same vision that I see—not through the transference of thought, but as their own individual unfoldment. They tell me they have been able to meditate and hear the still, small voice and receive impartations.

If they can do that in these few days, think of what you can do if you will stick to this path—to the teaching, not to the teacher—of the universal Christ manifest as your individual mind and soul and body. Do not forget that we do not leave the body out of this. It is a fine traveling companion!

Watch the consciousness of the presence of God open your consciousness to the inflow of good. Do not outline in what form it will come or through or with whom or where or when. Open your consciousness to God and let it become evident or manifest. "Not my will, but thine, be done."[4] And, please, not with mental work. "Not by might, nor by power, but by my spirit."[5] Every word of truth, remember, is a treatment. You do not have to be repeating and affirming it. Every word of truth you entertain and let drop is a treatment! Not by might–the effect of truth itself is the might.

~5~

THE NATURE OF ERROR

GOD IS ALL! Nevertheless we are faced every day and almost every hour of every day with error in some form. It is for that reason we come together to study metaphysics or spiritual truths. The object of our study is, of course, coming into oneness with that spiritual life, coming to that point where we are actually able to contact the mind that was in Christ Jesus and thereby have the infinite power, guidance and direction, love and protection of that universal mind and soul. It is natural for us to agree that one reason we would love that, is because it does eliminate the errors of human sense.

Now, two things are necessary in that spiritual living. One is this contact, this ability to be one with the mind that was in Christ. The other, which is the letter of truth, is the ability to know our relationship to God and to understand the nature of error. In order to be free of discord, let us never forget that it is necessary for us to know the nature of error. Now, in our meditation we are going to be so consciously one with God that eventually error never comes near us, it fades away automatically even as we approach it. Until that time, let us not hesitate to talk about the nature of error and what we are to do about it as we see evidences of it.

We know that error isn't a reality. That is the basis of our understanding. Everyone in this room, regardless of what school of metaphysics he comes through, has accepted, if only intellectually, the unreal nature of error. But in the working out of problems it becomes necessary to go as far as can be with this understanding of the unreal nature of error, so that we can meet it and dissolve it instantaneously. So, before we touch on meditation and the results of meditation, I am going to talk on the nature of error.

To begin with, when error appears to us, it appears as a person or as a condition or as a place. In the same way, when good appears to us, it appears as a person, a place, a condition. When I look out here, all that is actually here is God, but God appearing as persons, God appearing as cooperation—love, joy, peace, dominion. It is all God appearing *as:* God appearing as person, as friend, as teacher, as student; God appearing as light, truth, love in all its infinite and individual forms.

Now, when this thing called error (which isn't a thing but an appearance) appears, it likewise appears as person or place or thing or condition. Error never appears as error; it always appears in some form that will fool you. If error would only appear as error, we'd all be free. If it would only say to us, "Let us steal a diamond ring," oh, we'd be so safe from it, we'd never give in! If it would only say to us, "Let us commit adultery," oh, we'd be so safe from it!

It doesn't appear that way. It appears as a beautiful diamond attracting us, or a handsome man, or a beautiful woman tempting us. And we do not see that it is the error tempting us. All that we see is that beautiful form that it appears to be, that it appears as. It is the same way with disease. Disease appears to us as some kind of localized condition, and that's what fools us. We go to work on that condition, thereby we almost become one with it! At least, we make it a reality.

Now, when the metaphysician who is alert sees a form of good, like a good person or a generous person or a kindly or philanthropic person, the wise metaphysician will instantly say, "You don't fool me. That's God! Those are the qualities of God appearing in or as or through this person." And so you won't get tangled up in personality, and you won't get so completely tangled up in attraction for a person that the loss of that person or his disappearance can almost drive you mad—or a fall from grace might so disappoint you it could cause heartbreak. The wise metaphysician, even while appreciating a good person will, at the same time, look behind the form and say, "Oh, yes! But I happen to know that it is God appearing as you. It is really the presence of divine mind, the presence of love, expressed as you." You don't say it out loud but that's your thought and that's the consciousness you live in. When everything of a good nature is appearing to you, you immediately translate and say, "I recognize you—it is God appearing to me as good."

But, on the other hand, we must be equally alert when error appears. Now error is not a person. Error is never a person. And to immediately work on an evil person is to get yourself so mixed up in it that you'll have a hard time ever bringing out a healing. In the same way, error is never a diseased person, either. It appears that way, but it isn't that, and if you work on the disease of the person, ultimately you are going to find your healing work isn't really good. It isn't instantaneous, it isn't even quick. It isn't satisfactory. When you

are confronted with an evil person or a sick person or
situation, you must learn that just as you translated the
good person back into God, you must translate this evil
person or condition back into impersonal error. And
now I am going to show you the method of doing that.

Remember, we used the illustration of the streetcar
tracks. You see the tracks coming together in the distance, but you immediately translate that, knowing there
is no such evil condition, but merely the appearance,
due to finite eyesight. And so you have wiped out the
fear of the wrong condition of the tracks; you have
wiped out any sense that there might be danger because
they seem to come together in the distance.

In the same way you remember the illustration of the
hypnotist with his victim and his (imaginary) white
poodle. I, sitting out here in the audience, know right
well when that man asks for help to get rid of his white
poodle that I mustn't give him help to get rid of his
white poodle—otherwise I would be in the same state of
mesmerism that he is in. The mere fact that I am not
hypnotized makes me see that there is no white poodle
there. The claim isn't white poodle, the claim is hypnotism. The minute I know that, that man is free. Why is
he free? Because the error has been uncovered, it has
been seen, it has been recognized for its nothingness.
You know hypnotism can't produce a white poodle, can
it? It can only produce an illusory appearance, and
nobody is going to be afraid of that. The fear comes only
while we believe there is a white poodle there.

Now, inasmuch as we have no condition of disease in
the world, we have no condition of sin, because if we
have, rest assured, we haven't got a God. Don't ever
believe that there is an infinite power called divine love

and that there is a sin or a disease in the world or you'll be in a bad fix! You can't have both—you've got to make your choice. Either you have come into the assurance, the realization that there is a God, a principle of the universe, or else you are going to be battling sin, disease and death all your life. But, once you have seen that God is the substance, the law and the form of all being, then you must agree that sin, disease and death, lack and limitation, unemployment, homelessness—all of that—is illusion.

Through the centuries in which the human sense has built up what we call *materia medica*, a theological belief and other material beliefs, these beliefs have become so strong that they act on us like hypnotism. In other words, sit in a draft and catch cold. Why? Well, the draft can't give you a cold. I've even had a physician admit, after he thought it out, that your body really doesn't know whether you are out in the open air or whether the air is coming in through a window or a door, and that there isn't any part of the body that can ever know that, or be affected by it. If you do get a cold from sitting in a draft, it all must be because the mind in some way has accepted that kind of law.

Now, inasmuch as a newborn babe can get in a draft and catch cold, it must mean, not that the newborn babe has that thought, but that the thought, this belief, is so universal, so powerful, so almost mesmeric, it impinges itself on that babe almost the moment it is born. The babe becomes the victim of that which it doesn't even know.

For that reason in this work, we have agreed to use some words (very inadequate words, we admit), the only words I know so far to describe the real nature of error: we have agreed to use the words "hypnotism" or "mesmerism" or "suggestion," so that when you see a person in sin or disease, immediately lift your thought and say, "I can't be fooled! That's the appearance, but actually it's nothing but a hypnotic suggestion, a mesmeric suggestion, or a universal belief that is appearing to me as a sick person or a sinful person." Then you will have an instantaneous or quick healing.

As you are meeting with error in your existence—and you are meeting it in your own body or business or through your patients—as long as you are meeting some form of error, you might as well know what it is you are meeting so that you will know how to handle it. Probably when you get to that degree of oneness with the Christ-consciousness, you will be able to forget this. You will be able to drop out of your thought, entirely, that you ever knew—or cared—what the nature of error was. It is relatively unimportant once you are completely one with that mind that was also in Christ Jesus. It may be that some of you, even at this moment, are on a spiritual level to the degree that when you close your eyes and go to the center of your being and find yourself one with God, all phases of error and discord will disappear without the word "error" coming to your thought.

As a rule I have found it helpful to me, when I am first presented with any form of error, when a patient writes me, or telephones me or comes to the office, for me to realize quickly, "I'm not dealing with a person or a condition. I am only dealing with a suggestion that wants to get in and make me do something about it." When I've done that, I've done all that's necessary in the way of treatment. After that I can sit down, find my peace, get right to the center of God-consciousness, and go on from there.

Unless I do the other first, the temptation is apt to come in, "This is a pretty kettle of fish! What am I going to do about a serious disease like this? Or what am I going to do with a person this far gone in sin? Or with this person so close to death?" And of course you know this temptation is particularly strong when elderly people come to us, because there you have the whole world's temptation to believe, "Oh, what can you expect?" It is right there that you have got to be alert to realize that in the kingdom of God there are no such things as newborn babes or elderly people. Everything from the newest born babe to the oldest individual on earth is nothing but the presence of God suggesting itself to you in time and space.

I recently wrote a letter to some people experienced in truth who were battling this condition of disease in elderly people, and in the letter I wrote that it would not be bad to remember a sentence that Mrs. Eddy wrote many, many years ago: "Mortality is a myth"–that includes all mortality, from infancy to old age–it is all a myth. Then perhaps you won't feel it natural for older people to be sick and younger ones to be well.

Every one of us must express the fullness of God. All that the Father has is ours. "Son, all that I have is thine."[1] And this wasn't addressed to a person of any particular age, either. So when you are presented with cases, as you have been and will be again, even cases of unborn children and cases of newborn children, cases in middle age and cases in old age, remember clearly that we are not dealing with person, place or thing. On the positive side, we are dealing with God appearing as individual being, and it is just as much God at one hundred years of age as it is at twenty-two. God appearing as individual

being! And on the negative side we are dealing with
appearance, with mortality, with a myth, with a suggestion of a selfhood apart from God. Therefore, do not let
yourself be trapped into treating a person or a disease
and watch the miracle that happens in your healing
work. Heretofore, we have believed that we were
dealing with sick people or sinful people. Now, stop that
and watch the miracle. Remember, this must prove itself
in your practice because it is a universal truth.

There is no such thing as error and there is no use
trying to account for error. But you can say that it
certainly is an appearance coming to you, it is a temptation coming to you to believe in a selfhood apart from
God. Whether you choose to say, "Oh, well, this is
hypnotism suggesting what appears to be a white poodle
or this is a temptation to believe in a selfhood apart from
God," or whether you find other terms that you like
better, so long as you get the essence of what I'm saying
and know that, never will you be called upon to heal a
sick or sinning person. There is no such thing in the
kingdom of God. And don't forget that heaven and earth
are not two different places. There is no use saying, "Oh,
I know there is no such thing in heaven, but what about
earth?" Heaven and earth are the same place. Earth is
our mortal concept of heaven. Heaven is our real
awareness of the earth. In other words, heaven is the
earth correctly understood.

Never forget that this life of yours is God and if it
appears to me to be young or old, sick or well, evil or
good, that is just God appearing falsely to me–and I am
the one who must reinterpret the scene. Now we have
two ideas: right identification which means God appearing as individual life; and sin, disease and death, which

is nothing more or less than God being wrongly interpreted by us. So the next word, after right identification
is reinterpretation.

Right identification—which means the one appearing
as many, or God, life, appearing as individual being; and
then reinterpretation—which means looking right at sick,
sinning, human, dying men and reinterpreting that to
see, inasmuch as God is all, that this is part of the allness
of God which is being mis-seen, coming to me as a false
suggestion, which I must reinterpret. Now, you must
carry with you these two words, from morning to night
and night to morning. Two words: right identification
and reinterpretation.

Reinterpret everything you see, hear, taste, touch and
smell. Reinterpret it back to its original state which is
Godhood. Be sure that you practice right identification,
knowing that all that appears to you is God appearing as
the individual man, woman or child, God appearing as
the plant, animal, the crops, and then knowing what the
human eye sees is the misconception of that divine idea.
What the human eye sees, what the human ear hears, is
the false picture presented by this thing I call hypnotism
or suggestion. It is the same thing that presents the two
tracks coming together in the distance, or presents the
sky sitting on the mountain, or presents the imaginary
white poodle. I really do not care what name or term
you find for it. Just be sure you are willing not to get so
absolute that you won't reinterpret what is appearing to
you in the scene.

In the book, *The Infinite Way*, the most important
chapter for the metaphysician is "The New Horizon."
This chapter is the explanation of what I have just said:
the reinterpretation of what you behold. In other words,

it tells you clearly that the entire human picture is mesmeric suggestion. It is a suggestion coming to you of a selfhood apart from God. You are called on to reinterpret it.

What happens after you have done that for awhile? You don't have to *try* to do it any more. It becomes automatic. As you see people and events, you translate them, or reinterpret them. You really see them as they are, without any mental protest.

That is one reason why we need so little treatment in this work. Because, the very moment a person, place or thing presents itself to us, we immediately say, "I know you. God appearing!" Then, the second thing, "Oh, but how sick or sinful!" That we can reinterpret. We say, "That is but the false sense of God appearing. That is the suggestion, the human sense of things, and is purely illusory." As you learn not to fight it or battle it, you come into oneness with the reality and that's all there is to it.

Now, this subject of knowing the nature of error is one that has never been a pleasant one to teach in metaphysics. The average person doesn't like it. He would much rather spend the time talking about God and all the loveliness of God. I assure you that I am one of those who would much rather stick to the main theme of the Christ that liveth in me, than to go off on this other angle. But I have learned the danger of that. I have learned that there are too many people in the metaphysical world who are perfectly willing to talk about the allness of God and then see error eating them up! It is just what we were saying here the other night. We come across people indulging in various forms of error right in the metaphysical world. They say, "Well, it hasn't any power," yet they are indulging it so it must have some

power or they wouldn't be indulging it. Still they look
you right in the face and say, "Well, it has no power,
what are you afraid of?" It's getting the best of them, and
it would get the best of us too if we kept saying, "It has
no power—just power enough to attract me."

What's the use of all this nonsense of going around
saying, "There's no evil," while at the same time we
keep two or three telephone lines going so that people
who are sick can reach us. It isn't consistent, is it? Now,
when we arrive at that state of spiritual consciousness in
which we can look right out and never behold any form
of suggestion, that drops away. Then we no longer need
to think a thing about this.

Probably most practitioners, at some time or other,
are so lifted up in consciousness, that when people come
to them the error drops away and without their having
any conscious thought about anything. Perhaps some of
you remember the illustration of that at the Chicago
World Fair when Kate Buck had a man come to her
with a visible growth who asked her to talk to him about
God. He did not ask for treatment. She spent two hours
talking about God. The man left her office without
asking for or receiving further treatment. In the morning
the man's wife telephoned that the growth had entirely
disappeared.

You see, in that two hours Kate Buck had elevated
herself to such a state of spiritual consciousness that she
was not conscious any longer of what that man was
presenting to her. Of course, in that purified state of
consciousness, she did not have to declare, "This is
suggestion!" It was self-evident that it was only suggestion.

So I don't mean that it is always necessary for you to
absolutely make the statement, "Oh, this is suggestion,"

or "Oh, this is hypnotism and isn't person, place or thing." I don't mean that at all. I do mean, get it into your consciousness that any form of error is only suggestion and stop giving treatments to people or conditions. Then it doesn't make any difference if you never think of it again. Train yourself to know that you are never dealing with a sick or sinning person, you never have a disease to deal with. All you have are the universal beliefs!

Why, my own grandfather passed on with one of them. He was taken sick when he was sixty-nine. For awhile the family thought he would pass on and one day he said, "Please don't be fearful of my passing, I am not going to die. The Bible promised me three score years and ten and I will live to it." And he did. He passed on at seventy.

Yes! You see, we just accept these things at their face value and then we go out and demonstrate. Now, don't accept the suggestion of three score years and ten. And don't accept the doctor's suggestion that a disease is very dangerous or very serious. Remember, it is suggestion, and the chances are that after it is healed the doctor will say, "You know, I think my diagnosis was wrong!" So even the suggestion isn't so.

You can set aside any law of belief. You can't set aside a law of God. The law of God is life eternal. The law of God is, "All that I have is thine." All the eternality. All the immortality. You can't set that aside, but you can set aside the belief that you must die at any specific time, whether it is the doctor that says it, whether it is the Bible with its three score years and ten that says it, or whether it is the stars that say it. You can set that aside by becoming a law unto your own being

through the realization that yours is a God-given dominion. God gave man dominion over the things of the
earth, over the waters, over the stars, over the heavens.
God gave you–its own individualized being–dominion.
But, you must consciously exercise this. You can't sit
back and let those beliefs act upon you.

Now, remember: these beliefs, these universal beliefs,
whether medical belief, or theological belief, do act on
you until you consciously set them aside. In other words,
every day of the year you are growing older. Unless you
consciously are realizing, "My life is God and ageless,"
then you do come under this human belief about the
time of change of life. You'll respond in accord with
medical beliefs, unless you yourself consciously take
possession of your life through your God-given dominion and say, "No, my life is God! All the rest of this
belief about age and change–that's all medical belief or
suggestion and it does not have to operate in or upon or
through my consciousness. 'Thousands shall fall at my
left hand, tens of thousands at the right'[2] if they don't
want to take hold of this universal truth. Each one has
the right, either by choice or through ignorance, to go
through life in his own way."

You have the right to take hold of your own existence
and determine it. One way is to be sure that you know
when error appears, what it is, so that it does not fool
you. Don't let it make you accept a sick person or a
sinful person to try to reform or heal. Otherwise you will
be in the same boat he is in, it will be the blind leading
the blind.

The only thing that sets us apart from the man in the
street, the only difference between a practitioner and a
patient, is that the practitioner cannot be fooled into

believing you are a human being. The practitioner knows that regardless of appearances, it is God appearing as individual being, and the practitioner won't accept anything else. In the same way, the practitioner won't accept a sick person as a patient or a diseased person for a patient or a sinning person for a patient, but will say, "I know you! 'Get thee behind me, Satan!'[3] You are just a false concept tempting me into accepting you as reality. I know you so you can take off your false face."

By reinterpreting and by right identification, you really and truly come into a state of consciousness where life becomes not a mental process, but a looking out and seeing God and that all is well with the world!

~6~

MEDITATION

WE MUST CONSIDER MEDITATION at this point, because it will more and more play an important part in your life and, as a matter or fact, become very important. Meditation may be a practice that extends over a period of five minutes or five hours, or it can be an experience of seconds. To begin with, let us take up the subject of meditation as we would if we are not perfectly familiar with it. In other words, let's start in as if it were a new subject to us.

Now, you remember that on the first night I spoke about beginning the day with that part of *The Infinite Way* that gives us instructions about waking in the morning, to be found in the chapter entitled "Meditation." I hope you have been religiously following this, because it leads to this idea of meditation.

You see, the minute you awaken in the morning and realize, "I and the Father are one,"[1] you are meditating. That is going within and realizing the inner reality of being, and that's meditation. Any form of going within is meditation, especially when you have something to meditate on, and you do: you have, "I and the Father are one." And even if you declare this only once with your eyes closed, you meditate on that particular idea.

Now, if you sat down in your chair for a few moments
and realized or pondered the idea that "the wave is one
with the ocean, so I am one with God . . . as a sunbeam
isn't something separate and apart from the sun, but
really an emanation of the sun itself . . ." and so on, you
were meditating. You see, there is nothing of a secret or
occult nature about meditating–nothing of a secret
process–nothing strange or mysterious. Meditation is
nothing more or less than pondering some idea of
universal truth.

Now, let us suppose we are getting ready to leave
home and go about our business but we want some
meditation first. We are not going to take any of our
problems into the meditation at all. Our meditation is
merely the realization or conscious establishment of our
unity with God; therefore, we are not going to think
whether we are going to meditate for five minutes or
twenty minutes. We leave the element of time out
because it is apt to fool us; we are apt to begin thinking
of the end of the time instead of leaving it alone and
letting it work itself out. It may only be necessary to
meditate two or three or four minutes. On the other
hand, it may take six or seven or eight minutes to get the
feeling that must come with the end of meditation.

Start with some statement that you love, some statement that you would like to understand better–either a
scriptural statement or a metaphysical statement, and let
us see what happens with it. We will take the statement,
"I and the Father are one!" All right, that's the one that
comes. . . .

Now, just a word about posture. There is nothing
mysterious about posture, either–nothing of an mysterious or hidden nature that has to do with posture. There

is only one reason that we bring in the subject of posture and that's the common sense one of being comfortable. Meditation is most easily achieved when the body is in its most natural state and does not intrude into thought. If I sit in a straight chair like this, with my feet firmly on the floor, my back straight as the backbone is supposed to be—straight up, chin in—and both my hands resting on my lap, not resting on a chair where in a few minutes I am going to feel the wood pressing in, but in my lap, I am in a position where my body should not intrude itself into my thoughts. I should be able to maintain this position for five, six, ten, twenty minutes, without ever thinking about the body because I am in a perfectly normal and natural position. That is the only reason we speak of posture.

As you know, our Eastern friends sit on the floor, cross their legs, and the like. That is absolutely natural for them. Why? Because in the Near and Far East, few people ever sit on a chair; the floor is their natural place and sitting on the floor the most natural posture. In that position, the most natural thing is for the feet to be underneath the body, so their reason for sitting in that position has nothing to do with any mysterious powers. It has only to do with the naturalness of the posture in their countries.

Now we have taken the natural position and we have taken the idea that "I and the Father are one." We may repeat that a couple of times—"I and the Father are one." Then the thought comes, "*I*. . . . Well, really if there is only one *I*, that *I* is God. Just think, *I* and the Father are one. Then naturally all that the Father is, is one! And my being one with that, makes all of the Father one with me. It makes me one with all of the Father. . . ."

Now you see, what I am doing is just pondering this idea of I and the Father and what it means, so that I do not get into that horrible habit of making a quotation out of it, because saying "I and the Father are one," isn't going to do a thing for me! Once that idea unfolds in my consciousness, once I've tapped the terrific import of the meaning of "I and the Father are one," I have achieved immortality, eternality, health and wealth.

And so our meditation is really for arriving at the real meaning, the inner meaning of the statement, "I and the Father are one." Now, it may happen that we as beginners, can't keep that up very long. We lose the thread of it and we find ourselves thinking about whether we are missing our appointment at the office, or missing the bus or the train. The next thing we know, we are wandering.

At that point, you just gently bring your thoughts back to that statement, "I and the Father are one." Don't condemn yourself. Don't get impatient with yourself. Don't think that you're hopeless! Just pay no attention to this wandering of the mind, but gently bring it back and start again, pondering this idea. Or maybe by that time some other idea will have come to you, probably a better one for the moment. As many times as your thoughts wander from it, you gently come back to the idea again, with no impatience or anything of the kind.

In the same way, in this beginning state of ours, it isn't only that our thoughts wander, but another thing happens. Thoughts keep racing in and out, all kinds of undesirable thoughts. You may think they are your thoughts. They are not. They are just banging away at you. They come in and they disturb you; they distract you. Don't fight them; don't try to stop thinking them—you can't succeed. I'll tell you that and save you a lot of trouble. You'll never succeed in stopping your thinking, so let those thoughts come in and go out and do anything they want. You just hew to your center, to the particular quotation you are pondering. Let those other thoughts do what they want and don't bother with them.

There will come a time, as you continue in this practice, when those thoughts won't come in any more. That's all right. You have starved them out by neglect. You have made yourself so unreceptive to them by not fighting them that they won't bother to come back. I assure you, if you fight them, they will be there forever! Your fighting them is the very thing that keeps them there. "Agree with thine adversary whilst thou are on the way with them."[2] All of these wrong thoughts that keep coming in aren't dangerous, aren't harmful; nobody will know about them and they won't hurt you. Let them come, let them go. Pay no attention to them.

You are in meditation for one purpose. To ponder, "I and the Father are one," "My kingdom is not of this world[3]. . . . Thou wilt keep him in perfect peace whose mind is stayed on thee."[4] Take anything. Select your own quotation. Or maybe you won't have to—maybe you will get into the habit where something you need for that day will come to you and you will ponder that.

The main point I am making is that you have a central thought, a central quotation. You take it into meditation, not for the purpose of repetition, but for the purpose of pondering its real meaning, its inner meaning, getting the real light on it so that you never again use it as a mere quotation.

I can still remember how often I took in the statement, "Not by might nor by power, but by my spirit."[5]

I finally arrived at the place where it said to me, "Not by physical might nor by mental power, but by my spirit"–by just the reality of my own being. And as I told you, for eight months I practiced this five and six and eight times a day before I even arrived at the place of one speck of a second of peace and quiet within. But you won't go through that. The mere fact that I have done it is proof it can operate the same in you who have come into this consciousness.

This is a strange thing, too. You never have to go through the various stages of somebody else's development. You'll never have to be crucified. You'll never have to be persecuted. That all happened to Jesus and the martyrs and all those other people, but you don't have to go through that. You can start where they left off. You will never have to drive model-T Fords. You will never have to light your house with kerosene lamps. You can start right in at the highest point of development.

And so it is with metaphysical truths. You will not have to go through those horrible days of giving mental treatments and protecting yourself from mal-practice and worrying about what evil influences are coming to bear upon you. You can start at the highest level that has been revealed to consciousness, because all of the other people who went through that have paved the way for you. It is the same with meditation. You will find, I am sure, that before next week is over you will be telling me that you are having original ideas or original quotations coming to you. I mean original in the sense that I haven't given them to you, but that they have come directly to you and that you are able to settle down for a minute, or two or three or four, of peace.

Now, as you are pondering this quotation and utterly
disregarding human thoughts that come and go, do one
more thing. You have to do two things at once in this.
Keep this ear alert, as if you were going to hear something. It isn't because, in meditation, you actually do
hear something or that you necessarily must hear things.
It's only that the ear is our finite concept of hearing the
still small voice, that's all. It represents to us "a listening
ear." Now, a listening ear isn't physical at all. Just as we
are told, "those who have ears to hear . . . those who
have eyes to see,"[6] you know that has nothing to do with
the physical ear, nothing to do with the physical eye. So
when I say keep this ear open, it isn't that it makes any
difference whether you ever hear a voice or not. It is just
your human representation of the spiritual idea of
receiving, of receptivity. Thus, while pondering, while
meditating on this one idea, you also are keeping this ear
open—really a sign of receptivity.

Of course, there is another thing, too. If anyone
thinks that meditation has anything to do with resting or
falling asleep, he is going to soon find out that it is the
keenest state of alertness there is in the world! A person
who knows how to meditate will never fall asleep. As a
matter of fact, two, three, four minutes of meditation is
enough to drive away all the tiredness he may have had
from a whole day's work. Meditation, you see, is letting
in the divine spirit—God. That dispels every illusion of
sense.

Now, the reason I say not to limit meditation in time
is this: the very minute that it begins to be a bore or an
effort, stop it. Don't let it be an effort. Stop it. If it has
been only one and one-half minutes, be satisfied. Because if you have been holding the idea of God for but

a half minute, you have been opening your receptivity, you've started the inflow. You may not get an answer. You may get one six hours later or twelve days later. But you have opened consciousness to the inflow of truth.

Now, if you can do this, begin with meditation three times a day. Certainly twice–morning and night. And there isn't anybody on earth that can't do that because everybody gets up and everybody goes to bed. So everybody can spare an extra couple of minutes in the morning and an extra couple of minutes at night before they retire, even if they can't find one other minute during the day. But there are some of you who will find that between getting up in the morning and going to bed at night, there is another interval of two or three minutes. At that time you can retire or go to a restroom and give another minute or two for meditation. Don't make a mental effort of this! You are not going to get into the kingdom of God by force. You are never going to take heaven by any mental or physical power. It's a gentle oozing your way in.

So, if you will give two or three or four minutes to this little process, two or three times a day to begin with, it will stretch itself out. You may arrive at that place where you can sit in meditation for four hours and really feel when you were through that, "My, this ten minutes went around in a hurry!" That's individual. There are people who will never achieve that because they are not temperamentally suited to it. But everyone can achieve meditation for three, four or five minutes.

Now the reason I say that this is going to be increasingly important in your life is this. These two or three periods of meditation are contacting points, those points at which you touch God. But, they are going to lead to more than that. After this becomes an almost regular part of your existence, you are going to find, gradually, that you can meditate at any hour of the day or night; sometimes for a half-second and sometimes for minutes on end, even while driving your car, even while doing house work, even while sitting and talking to a person or a patient, or in between visits. You will find that without getting mystical or occult or anything else, you can learn to open your consciousness for just that second and become a state of receptivity.

Now, what happens is this: Once that line is open, once you have become a state of receptivity, your guidance, leading, direction and help flow continuously through you. It is as if you had opened up a line to God, and from that moment on, it just pours through as you need it. It appears as you need it. If you need direction, it says to you, "Don't go this way." If you need leading, it says, "Go that way." If you need money, it appears; if you need a parking space, it appears but not because you are merely demonstrating things.

It is like the illustration of Lake Erie and Niagara Falls. We cannot demonstrate Niagara Falls, but by having the consciousness of Lake Erie we can have Niagara Falls. And we needn't stop at one. With the consciousness of the ocean, we can have lots of Niagara Falls! But don't go trying to demonstrate Niagara Falls because that's apt to bring a sense of separation from Lake Erie. Once we have Lake Erie, we have Niagara Falls on the American side, on the Canadian side, and a few more, too. But let's be sure we have the consciousness of Lake Erie.

In the same way, let us never violate "seek ye first the kingdom of God and his righteousness and all these things will be added." Let us make meditation the tuning in, if you want to call it that, or *at-one-ment* with the divine source of being.

Let me put it this way. As humans we seem to be just so many feet tall and wide and pounds heavy and that's all of us. Now, we live by bread. The food we eat and the drink we drink, the air we breathe really constitutes us, as humans. But in our spiritual living we are told we do not live by bread alone. What do we live by then, if we don't live by bread alone? By "every word that proceedeth out of the mouth of God."[7] That doesn't mean quotations, or affirmations, or denials. It means, really, every idea—every item of consciousness, every thrill of intelligence and love—that's what we live by!

But how do we get it? As humans we haven't got it at all. Here we are—this is all there is to us! It is only when we have opened this contact to the infinity of being, to the ocean of knowledge, to the ocean of love—from that moment on we are not living by bread alone. We are living by bread—oh, yes, and cake, too! But we are not living by bread alone. We have the divine inspiration, the wine that Jesus spoke of, the water that Jesus spoke of, the bread that Jesus spoke of. Do you remember how he told the people, "Your fathers did eat manna in the wilderness, and are dead."[8] Surely, they ate the bread that Moses gave them, that was bread for their hunger. But, he said, "This is the bread that came down from heaven . . . he that eateth of this bread shall live for ever."[9]

Now, Moses gave them water, too, remember? He made it come out of rocks. But that wasn't it. That was improved humanhood. That is just as though I would sit here and demonstrate another twenty-five or fifty dollars a week income for you. That would be like Moses' demonstration of increased good. But if I can show you how to open your consciousness to the inflow of God, then whatever of increased good comes to you isn't just an increase of humanhood, it's the Divine itself, and that flow never stops! That's why you'll never hunger once that bread comes to you.

I remember my first year in the work. When I first went into this work I did like most of the practitioners I knew. I had statements made, and a book showed absent treatments and present treatments and office treatments and all the rest of it. At the end of the month, I religiously tabulated all of these and sent out bills. Well, that went on for seven months until the realization came that I wasn't living from God, I was living from these Joneses and Browns who were paying their bills. And what would happen if they didn't pay? That was a poser. Then I would be in a fix. It was then that I stopped sending bills.

I began to realize that if I could demonstrate that by the love of God alone my bills were paid in any month, I was safe for life; the love of God could never be taken away from me. You'll never stop that flow once you have contacted it, and that's the secret! Once you touch this Christ—once you touch this center of consciousness—once you open your consciousness to the inflow of the health of God, of spiritual supply—you'll never again hunger. You'll never again have demonstrations of supply to make.

In family life, too, we won't need to worry whether divorce courts work. We won't need them any more. Once we've touched that idea of the love that comes from God, we will find it in wife and husband and child–but only when we are getting it through the idea which we bring to bear through meditation. It's always through that meditation.

And so I say meditation is important; not merely to sit down for a few moments, for I know the day will come when it won't mean a thing that you sit down or that your body is comfortable. You will be driving your car and meditating. You will be sleeping at night and meditating. You will be sleeping in God-consciousness instead of the comatose brain. That's the way it will be. That takes care of things.

You see now that in this meditation you will receive ideas of truth, ideas which exteriorize themselves in what we call tangible form, as bread on the table or as healing or as truth that dispels error. It even reveals to you the nature of error; it will make it appear as illusion, so that you won't even have to think of it in that light, it will come through in its own way. So meditation is for us one of the most important things to develop. Only don't try to press; don't try to exert mental effort. It's not by might nor by power. It's by the gentle spirit.

~ 7 ~

TEACHING THE MESSAGE

FOR THE BENEFIT OF THOSE who are having the experience of imparting some of this to patients or students, I want to speak for a little while on what we may call teaching *The Infinite Way* and *Spiritual Interpretation of Scripture*. By that I don't mean class teaching. By the time that any of you are conducting a class on it, we will have a special class to bring that type of work to a focus. What I mean though, is that if you have a patient or someone coming to you and you are trying to bring about a healing and at the same time introduce them to the subject of spiritual truth from this standpoint, I want to give you some hints along the way.

The first thing that must be brought out to the one who either has little or no metaphysics, or the one who is coming from some other school of metaphysics into this, is of course our meaning of terms like "soul," "Christ," and the difference between prayer and treatment. You know that in *Spiritual Interpretation of Scripture* I have made it clear that to my sense, treatment and prayer are not synonymous.

Treatment refers to the letter of truth, the statements of truth that we may make to ourselves as reminders of the truth of being. Treatment may be our conscious

97

realization, through either the spoken word or through silent thought, meditation, introspection, of the truths of being. But prayer would only begin when we had completed thinking or making statements or reviewing thoughts or ideas.

In other words, in our work the main point is that there is not God and men; probably this approach is unique in that. You cannot give a treatment to men, because in this approach we haven't any men separate and apart from God. Therefore, what the metaphysical world terms men we term God and man, or God appearing as man. Therefore it would be an impossibility for a practitioner to give a treatment to a man or a woman or a child if he understands clearly that all there is appearing as man, woman or child, is God–the one life, the one mind the one soul and spirit–that even the body of that individual is the temple of the living God.

Strange as it may seem, our first work with the young student is bringing to light that God is the mind of the individual; God is the life, the soul and the spirit, and that God is even the substance of the body of the individual claiming for the moment to be patient or student.

Now, while there is not a special chapter on that in either *The Infinite Way* or *Spiritual Interpretation of Scripture,* there are enough references in both those books to make up a chapter or a lesson on that particular subject. When I was assembling *The Infinite Way* and *Spiritual Interpretation of Scripture,* my work was all being done with students and patients who had known my work for so many years that I never thought of the chapter "God"! I know now that eventually we will have to have a chapter in which we will bring out oneness. Meanwhile you will have to make a chapter for yourself.

In the same way, last night we agreed on what Christ-consciousness is. To the average metaphysician Christ still is an unknown factor. I don't mean the name and I don't mean the fact that Christ is the spirit of God. What I mean is that it is more a term than it is really and truly the understanding of one's individual Christhood–that one's own real being is that Christ, that Christ is one's own consciousness when it has been purged of love, fear and hate or error of any nature. When we no longer love, fear or hate error in any form, we are Christ-consciousness.

Too many of us leave our patient and student in the belief that Christ or Christ-consciousness is something separate and apart from our own being, that it is something which might be attained. As a matter of fact, it might be attained, that is correct. But it might be attained only in one way: through our recognition of the nature of error which causes us to lose our love for it, our hate for it and our fear for it. So just as we have to bring God appearing as men into real conscious knowledge with the individual, we also have to bring the idea of Christ as Christ-imminent, as Christ of our own being, as Christ of our own consciousness. Otherwise you still have patient or student with God separate and apart, or the Christ separate and apart.

Now, of course, judging from my own experience, the most misunderstood word in the entire *Unity Metaphysical Dictionary* is the word "soul." Rarely do you meet a person in this work (I don't mean practitioners, I mean average patients and students) who has caught the vision of the word soul. And soul is so important that without it we haven't quite caught spiritual vision.

We know, of course, that we have physical senses; we call them the five senses: seeing, hearing, tasting, touching and smelling. We know those are the five finite senses, sometimes called metaphysically "the unreal senses." As a matter of fact, they are our misinterpretation of one word: *Consciousness.*

If I see you, I am conscious of your presence through sight. If I hear you, I am conscious of your presence through hearing. And of course, I can smell you and touch you and taste you, but all that is happening is that I am conscious of you. Therefore, these five senses are really only one sense and that one is consciousness. These are just five different facets of the activity of consciousness. As you think that over, you will see how very true it is that consciousness is the oneness, the *real one* faculty, and of course it is spiritual. The five physical senses are but the finite sense of one spiritual activity—consciousness. Consciousness finitized.

Now then, inasmuch as we here do not deny the body and do not deny the senses, we have to account for them. As we said last night, by right identification or reinterpretation we find we really have these activities of consciousness—which humanly we call seeing, hearing, tasting, touching and smelling—only instead of five there are seven. We have the faculty of intuition. Then we have the faculty of consciousness—without any thought process or any other process, it is actually silence. In that silence, which is the ultimate, we are alive in God, experiencing only God acting (or God conscious) through or as individual me and you.

However, we will call the activity of consciousness, soul senses, rather than five physical senses. Without eyes we are able to see. Now, that is not far-fetched—it is an accomplished fact. I have done it repeatedly and can do it at will. It involves the development of the soul senses. For instance, in experimenting with it years ago in developing that sense, I found that the time came when I could be in a dark room in the country at midnight, no lights around at all, blindfold myself, and in a few minutes I could see every detail of the room and I could see outside the room. That was because consciousness was operating without the limitation of physical eyes.

Hearing the "still small voice"[1] is just another facet of the same thing. Don't deny what I have said about seeing without eyes, or you will deny that you have ever heard the still small voice. That is just another activity in the same direction. It's hearing without ears; it's hearing without the faculty of hearing.

Now I know this first-hand because it happened to a member of my family. A member of my family was a musician and through an illness became stone deaf. It was discovered that both eardrums were broken and that never again would he hear. One of his relatives, who was just becoming interested in Christian Science, asked him to have treatments. He had one treatment, and from that day to this he has perfect hearing. But he still has no eardrums. The man, on account of his work (he is no longer a musician but in engineering), has had to have many physical examinations, especially during the war. Each time he is told, "You don't hear! That's impossible!" But he does. And he hears without any hearing aid. Evidently it was a practitioner of high consciousness who opened up the soul sense of hearing—hearing without eardrums.

In the same way, perhaps you know that in 1931 Brown Landone was told that he could not possibly live more than two hours. He had collapsed in Pennsylvania

Hotel, New York City, was carried to a room, and physicians were called in while he was still unconscious. They declared that he wouldn't live two hours. When they x-rayed him they discovered he had no entrance, whatever the technical term of it is, to the heart; with age it had worn out. He was then over eighty. Without this function, no man could live even minutes, certainly not over two hours. When he became conscious they told him he had a short time left and to get his things in order, if he could, as quickly as possible. He said, "If I have only two hours, I am going to spend them at my desk getting the important work done."

He got up. The next day he was still at the desk, still working. That went on. Several times the doctors were in to examine him and each time they said it was a miracle but certainly he had not two hours longer to go on. And that went on until three years ago—from 1931! He never again knew a sick moment. He never did develop that part of his heart, he just went on without it.

He had come to the place of knowing that life is God—or—God is life, and has nothing to do with what we call physical formations. When he went, you will re- member, he did not go through disease or by accident. He went only because he felt the time had come, that his call had come to do some other work. He turned to his secretary and said, "I am leaving you." Then he sat down and left, without ever having had a sick moment. He was then ninety-seven years of age, plus.

Now, none of these things are impossible if life has been lifted in your consciousness above the physical plane. Don't think for a minute that you, as practitioner, can give a treatment and have a person physically hear without ears or live without a heart. You can't do that any more than the doctors can. But if you catch this glimpse of life as God, then you are no longer living in a body, or through a body. Your body is then merely the vehicle. Your life is within or as your consciousness, and that is completely independent of physicality.

Should you feel like denying this, then you must accept the doctrine that life and consciousness end with the grave because you haven't got your ears and your legs and your feet with you after that. And if consciousness and life cannot go on independent of what we call this physical form, then of course you've got extinction at the grave side. You can have your choice. Accept what I am telling you or agree that your belief in immortality is going to be badly shaken.

Now, for this reason then, everyone in this work should study the word *consciousness*. Again I am sure there is a lot on that in the Unity Metaphysical Dictionary that is very good. Consciousness and soul—you must know them. Soul is the seat of those faculties which we interpret as physical organs and functions and physical faculties or physical senses. So all of us should know soul and consciousness. As a matter of fact, the day will come when, if you know enough about consciousness, you can leave everything else alone. The word consciousness, and the spiritual understanding of it, contains all the knowledge that is to be known about God, man and universe.

A minute ago we were back on that treatment and prayer. I explained treatment from our standpoint, but I didn't continue with prayer:

Prayer is that which takes place when we are through with the treatment and sit there just a little bit longer with that listening ear and receive an impartation—receive a message or a feeling, receive an awareness from within. That is prayer. Why? Prayer is the word of God. Man doesn't speak the word of God. God speaks the word of God; but, he speaks it to our individual consciousness, or *within* our individual consciousness. Therefore, those who have developed the listening ear, the attitude of receptivity, are those who receive the word of God, called prayer. That results in healing, reformation or any change necessary to what is called the outer picture.

Remember that we started with the declaration that there is no change in the outer scene until there has been a change in consciousness. Well, what change can there be unless something higher than the consciousness we have been holding enters to change us? And where does it enter from? Our thinking mind? No! We had that all the time.

We have to resort to something higher than the thinking mind. Very often we meet with situations in which we are told, "Oh, if you only had a better disposition, or if you just overcome impatience, if you only get rid of this or that, then you would get a healing!" But tell me, how do you overcome impatience or get rid of intolerance or injustice? How do you become more grateful? Well, you just don't if you are looking to your humanhood to do it for you. If that were possible, you would have done it long ago.

Your humanhood will not improve your humanhood. You have got to go higher. Therefore, it is only a spiritual sense, or the Christ, by which a person can be improved. Even if you could make a person a better human, you would have done nothing toward spiritualizing him. Never forget that. A better human is a better human, he is not spiritual consciousness. Therefore, to tell a person, "Oh, if you would just get rid of jealousy, if you would only get rid of hate." "Yes, but how do you get rid of it?" he might say. "I'd just love to get rid of it!" Well, there isn't any way, except by will power, and when you have done that you risk the fact that you may be just damming it up and it will break out again at another time or in another place. But the introduction of the Christ into individual consciousness will destroy jealousy, hate, enmity, injustice, dishonesty, immorality, sensuality; they can all be overcome by the introduction of the Christ.

How is that accomplished? In this work it is accomplished in many ways. Sometimes it comes through reading metaphysical literature or scriptural works. Sometimes just some statement at the right time registers in a person's consciousness and it makes him over anew. Sometimes it is, as I have told you of my own experience in 1928, meeting an individual of such high consciousness that when he touches you, he wipes out your whole human past—that part of it that you wanted wiped out.

It happens over and over that when people come to a practitioner who is in a high spiritual state or is normally of high spiritual consciousness, they automatically feel their fear drop away or they feel their antagonism or their hate or enmity or dishonesty or sensuality, just fade out! That is because they have been touched by the Christ of the individual called practitioner, teacher or lecturer. Sometimes, merely through the reading of this literature, the individual can do it himself. It either suddenly or gradually brings about a change in his entire nature. It does that because it is introducing Christ into human consciousness. Any way in which an individual is brought into the conscious presence of the Christ serves as the avenue through which human improvement takes place.

The subject of error should be very lightly touched on with the young student, and never to the depths we have taken it up in some of our work here, until he is well prepared for it. It is not an easy subject, especially until the practitioner or teacher himself has really mastered it. Like most other subjects, if you don't know it yourself, you have a hard time imparting it, even if you memorize all the words.

Metaphysical teaching or spiritual teaching is not the transfer of thought or words from one individual to another; it is the impartation of consciousness, of spiritual and uplifted consciousness, from one to another. And in the imparting or lifting up of that consciousness, all of this knowledge takes place.

The thing that we must be careful of in preaching is never to tell a patient or a student anything in the nature of a quotation or a cliché until we have, at least, demonstrated it in some degree. There is nothing worse in this work than hollow phrases, hollow statements, clouds without rain. That is one of the things we are most careless about. We are apt to be so smug in our wonderful statements of metaphysics, like, "Oh, you know it isn't real!" Of course he doesn't know it isn't real! The patient would have been healed if he knew that—you would never have to say it! We really make too many statements to our patients and students that we ourselves haven't mastered. Of course, we have authority for our statements, because Jesus or some metaphysical authority said it. Of course Jesus said it, but along the line we ourselves must catch some grasp of it. Then we find that the statements are really our own consciousness and our patient understands them and accepts them immediately. They are very apt to reject a cold statement from us, a statement that we are making but haven't, in a measure, demonstrated.

I have spoken much on the subject of spiritual integrity and lest anyone believe that I was speaking of human good, I want to dwell on that for a moment. Human good is not what I mean by spiritual integrity; one could be humanly perfect and not measure up to the standard of spiritual integrity. Spiritual integrity is living up to one's understanding of spiritual truth and living the Christ ideal. Now, that doesn't mean living a good human life or being a good moral person. I want to illustrate just what I do mean so that there is no mistake on the subject.

We believe, mostly, that the thought I am thinking within myself is secret and that you don't know it. That isn't true. Even if you are not a mind reader you will see very quickly that you do know. It was Emerson who told us, "What you are shrieks so loudly, I cannot hear what you are saying." And that's the truth about us. What we are within our own being becomes so much a part of our consciousness that if we were to say something opposite, nobody would believe us.

Now suppose I say, as a spiritual truth, "There is only one self . . . there is only one life," and yet, when some occasion arises, I lie a little or cheat a little. Who am I lying to and who am I cheating since there is only one self? And who am I hiding it from since there is only one mind and one life? No, as a good human I might go through life without ever cheating you of a nickel, but that would not be spiritual integrity. That would just be human goodness.

Spiritual integrity is the realization of the one self as the self of me and the self of all men, as the one mind

and the one life, as the mind and life of me and of all
men. Therefore, the interests of one are the interests of
all acting and living. That's living up to spiritual integrity
because I am making my thought and action conform to
my understanding of oneness. You see?

Suppose I accept, spiritually, the teaching that "All
that the Father hath is mine,"[2] and then I envy somebody else something of theirs. You see how I am violating my own spiritual integrity? I am not violating the
person I envy. He is not affected by it at all. I am
violating my own conviction that all that the Father has
is mine because I am not believing it—I am double-
minded. I am saying in one breath, "life is one," yet I am
setting up two: myself and the fellow I am envying or
cheating or defrauding.

In other words, spiritual integrity means living up to
the Sermon on the Mount: "Do unto others as you would
have them do unto you."[3] Only live up to that, not for the
sake of being a good human, but because you realize that
the other self is you—and you are that other self.

Now, if you always maintain this oneness in your
consciousness and act it out, you are maintaining your
spiritual integrity and if you never said a word to a
person, if you never preached a sermon on honesty or
integrity or loyalty or anything like that, they would feel
those qualities emanating from you. How could they
help it if that is your state of consciousness, if that is what
you are? You see what I mean?

Let us never indulge thoughts or acts that violate our
teaching of one self. How about criticizing and judging
and condemning the other fellow? Well, we are doing it
to ourselves and it will come back to us. Oh, don't you
ever worry that our errors won't come back to us! And

that is an error—not the act of judging or condemning; but the act of violating our own understanding that there is only one, and that we are judging and condemning our own being. Now, when we really accept this spiritual or metaphysical teaching of oneness, of the one true self, of one mind as the mind of every individual, as one life, one soul, one spirit—and live it—we are ushering in the millennium. We are really bringing about the time when there can be no war. We will even do away with lawsuits because in this inner conviction, in this inner understanding of oneness, we could not possibly act or think or do to another that which we would not do to our own being. Why? Because we would know that the self of the other is the self of our own being.

Is that pretty clear? In *Spiritual Interpretation of Scripture*—and I am going back now to that subject of teaching or explaining it to those who come to us—remember that the basis of it is that we are infinite spiritual consciousness embodying the universe within ourselves. That means embodying even the scriptures of the world within ourselves so that every character, every event of the Bible, is a character, an event, a quality or an activity of our own consciousness. So, in reading *Spiritual Interpretation of Scripture*, please read carefully with that in mind so that it is clear to you that what you are teaching from that book is that we must so live as to gradually weed out or overcome the erroneous traits of character represented by certain characters in the Bible. We turn our thoughts continuously to such as Moses or Elijah or Jesus, who are lights leading us out of the density of our false self, out of the bondage to sense, into the heritage of spiritual freedom.

~ 8 ~

ORDINATION

I AM GOING TO READ SOME NOTES that I made last night. No, I guess it was this morning; they began about three thirty and ended at five.

You took last night's lesson on "error and its nature" so beautifully that tonight I feel that I can give you your freedom; I can give you your freedom from what Jesus called "the world" or "this world." If you can receive this freedom tonight, it will be your holiest night on earth.

I give you two statements from the Master: "My kingdom is not of this world,"[1] and, "I have overcome the world."[2]

In the history of the world, only three men are known to have discovered the complete secret of life of their own accord. These men are Lao-Tzu of China, about 600 B.C.; Buddha of India, about 550 B.C.; and Jesus of Nazareth. Through Jesus, the full revelation came to the beloved disciple John on the Isle of Patmos.

Through Jesus, I received it in an unfoldment, first from the statement in the Bible, "My kingdom is not of this world." "My kingdom is not of this world" became the subject of my meditation for many months. I did not choose it, it clung to me. Then, "I have overcome the world." Finally came the realization of the meaning of

111

these statements. I have never known this to be taught
since it was received by John, except in his own veiled
writing. If you can receive it tonight, God has indeed
blessed you beyond all living men and women.

Friends, to overcome the world means to overcome
or rise above all sense of desire; to be free of world
attraction; to achieve being in the world but not of it; to
attain freedom from bondage to personal ego; to understand the spiritual world and thus gain freedom from the
false sense of God's universe. As we humanly see this
world, we are seeing God's heaven, but seeing it
"through a glass darkly." To overcome this world means
to rise above the human, finite, erroneous sense of this
world, and see it as it is.

John told us, you remember, that in that day we will
see him as he is and we will be satisfied. In this enlight-
ened consciousness we will see God face to face, even
though it is God appearing as you or as me, God appearing as individual man and woman.

The words I am speaking clearly show forth the
higher consciousness of life. But only as I can reach you
within and open your consciousness spiritually can you
come into the actual awareness of these words. This
experience here and now is spiritual baptism and the
Pentecostal experience of receiving the Holy Spirit.
From it you will emerge as men and women who have
seen through the mirage of sense testimony to the
underlying reality in which you actually live and move
and have your being.

This life you live is God "seen through a glass
darkly"–but now, in this instant, face to face. You can
now enjoy friendships, companionships, marriages,
business associations, without intense attachment. The

great victories of your friends or families will not unduly elate you and their failures will not too greatly disturb you. You will use dollars as a medium of exchange, but never again will you, who overcome this world, hate or fear or love them. You will handle dollars as you handle streetcar transfers—necessary and desirable activities of daily experience. You will always possess more than you need, without taking any anxious thought and without being concerned about dollars. Even their temporary absence will not embarrass or trouble you, because nothing in your world is dependent upon them. All that you require comes to you through grace as the gift of God.

In overcoming the world, you have overcome the beliefs which constitute this world, including the belief that man must earn his living by the sweat of his brow. You are joint heirs with Christ in God to all the heavenly riches, to every idea of infinite mind. In overcoming this world, you have lost your fear of your body; therefore it is free to live under God's law. You have overcome the world's beliefs about the body—that it is finite or material; that it lives by bread alone, or so-called material foods; that it must be catered to in any way. Bathe it, keep it clean inside and out, but drop all concern for it. It is in God's eternal keeping; it is living and moving and having its being in God-consciousness. Take no thought for your body, for it is God's concern to preserve and maintain the immortality of his own universe, including his body, which by reflection is your body.

There is only one body—here is the secret of secrets. There is only one body—the body of God, of which your body is the infinite reflection. As a reflection in a mirror exactly images forth your body, so does your body actually and exactly image forth the body of God. The

body you behold with your eyes is your individual concept
of the perfect reflection of the eternal body. What you
physically see as your body represents in thought your
idea of your body as it really is: the body of God reflected.
Your health is God's health reflected. Your wealth is God's
wealth reflected. Your family is the household of God
reflected as your consciousness of God's infinite reflection—individual being.

There is only one being and this one is God, and every
one represents your idea of that one individually expressed.
Your spiritual freedom means your freedom from the false
and often universal beliefs about the above subjects. You are
not any longer under the law of universal belief. You are set
free in Christ; that is, you have overcome or risen above the
beliefs about God's world. Therefore, you have overcome
this world, this false sense of the world. You now see the
world as it is and not as this world.

My peace I give thee, not as this world giveth, but the
spiritual peace I give you, the peace that passeth understanding, the peace that is not dependent upon a person
or outer condition. Nothing now in this world can affect
you who are free in Christ—in spiritual consciousness.
You will walk up and down in the world and come and
go freely and none of the world beliefs will kindle upon
you. The flames will not harm you; the waters will not
drown you. I have put my seal upon you. You are free.
Walk up and down, in and out. Spiritual law upholds
your being, your body, your business.

Tell no man what things you have seen and heard.
Do not explain or tell of your freedom from this world.
Move in and out among men, as a blessing—as a bene-
diction—as the light of the world. Let this life and mind
be in you which was in Christ Jesus. Be receptive; be

expectant; be always alert to receive inner guidance and direction and support. Keep attuned to your world within, yet fulfill all your duties without; fill all your obligations without, but keep alert within.

There are those here who have been called to God's work. It will be given you what to do and when. I have put my spirit upon you. This spirit will be seen and felt by men. It will not be you, but they will discern the spirit though they think of it as you.

My spirit will work for you and with you and through you and as you. It will work to accomplish my purpose. You will be my presence on earth. . . . I will not leave you, nor forsake you. In any appearance I will still be with you. Fear nothing of this world. . . . My guiding spirit is ever with you.

It is said of Lao-Tzu that when he was 1200 years old he grew weary because the world could not accept freedom from the grind of mortal living. He left the city to go out into the wilds of China and he was never seen again. Before going through the gate of the city, the gatekeeper, suspecting his purpose, asked him to write his teaching, which he did in just a short message. It is said of Buddha that he taught his disciples but found they could not quite realize the import of the message. One day he sent for them, bade them farewell, and left this plane. Jesus said, "Could ye not watch with me one hour?"[3] He also said, "If I go not away, the Comforter—the spirit of truth—will not come unto you,"[4] meaning that even the disciples had not grasped the import of his message.

Again, now, the message is repeated on earth to you. Will you also sleep? Let us take that into meditation now. . . .

~9~

MAKING THE ADJUSTMENT

NOW I WANT TO EXPLAIN that for tonight at least, I would like you to be very indulgent and very patient while we do a little adjusting. This is the first class I have ever had where we represent such varying states of consciousness. Because of that I want to make a little explanation and then bring together the adjustment of thought. Some here are widely experienced in metaphysical work from the standpoint of the Christian Science viewpoint; some are widely experienced in metaphysical work from the standpoint of other metaphysical approaches; others are almost beginners in metaphysical work and the spiritual approach to life.

So, when I talk I am reaching three different thought patterns and expecting all those three to understand the same thing in the same way and it can't be done. For that reason I think this evening should be devoted to bringing about a sort of equalization to see if everybody tonight, after a week of being together, can see what the approach is; then from here on, for everyone to understand the language we use and all that it means. For that reason I would like to start this evening off with questions—questions from you to me and, if necessary, some from me to you. We will see if we can, by means of these questions, answer some of the differences that may exist.

One reason for all of this is that I doubt there is any teaching now current that parallels this one. I don't mean by that, that there is any truth we are expressing or voicing that isn't included in all teaching; I don't mean that. I mean that the particular approach, the particular meaning of the truth or use of the truth or the purpose of the teaching is probably different from almost any other teaching in the metaphysical field.

To begin with, I will explain this. On the positive side, which is the side of right identification, we are standing wholly on the revelation of Jesus as given in the Gospel according to John. We are not deviating from that in any way, nor are we explaining it or elucidating it or in any way adding to it or taking from it. We are taking it absolutely as it stands in the revelation of Jesus as given in the Book of John. In other words, I am life eternal; I am the way, the truth and the light; I am the resurrection—which means, I am the power itself. Not—"I will be resurrected;" not—"there is some kind of law of God that's going to act on me." I am the resurrection! Not—"I will be supplied." I am the bread . . . I am the water . . . I am the wine. Now, when you stand on that, you stand on the revelation that you are infinite spiritual consciousness, infinite spiritual life itself, and, being infinite, all inclusive. Therefore, you must include within your own being every activity of being.

In taking that approach, you see what we are doing in contradiction to most of the metaphysical movements. We are saying, practically, that we can't help you demonstrate anything. All we can do is ask you to come into the realization of the infinite nature of your own being and let all things be added unto you. Right there, those of you who are familiar with metaphysical teachings must acknowledge that in that way, it is setting up for you a different approach to life. It is absolutely taking you out of the realm of being and idea or a reflection or an expression or an image or a son of God; it is taking you out of the realm of having to demonstrate something from the Father. So in that way, from those of you in this room who have the highest metaphysical teaching down to those who are beginning, this is a radical standpoint. You are taking the standpoint, "'I and the Father are one'[1]; therefore, I include all that the Father has and all that the Father is." Therefore, you are committing a sin every time you allow your thought to go out into the realm of "I desire, I want, I fear." You see?

Now, again, this is a very radical approach when it says, "Take no thought for your life, what you shall eat, what you shall drink, with what you shall be clothed."[2] You have to come into that realization wherein you can say, "My heavenly Father (which is my own infinite consciousness) knoweth what things I have need of, and it is his good pleasure to give me the kingdom."[3] Again, you cannot sit down and take thought. You cannot give yourself a treatment, even for supply. You see how radical this is and why it is natural that with only one week of it, we are not yet all in agreement in understanding the drastic approach that is given here? And that isn't the only deviation from the average teaching.

If you rightly caught the lesson of Friday night, you must understand that this teaching is not meant to give you something with which to demonstrate better or longer humanhood. This is a teaching that is meant to take you out of humanhood into the awareness of your spiritual identity. This is not a teaching to make your mind get things or do things for you. It is not a teaching to give you some power called "God" to bring you human things or human betterment. This is a teaching that is to make you be in the world but not of it. This is a teaching to bring the realization that, from the beginning of time, since before Abraham was, *I am*, and that I will be right here until the end of the world.

You see the absoluteness of the teaching? Not absolute good humanness, not absolute Science, but absolute realization of your spiritual identity. Again those who were here Saturday and heard the review, or whatever you call it, of the book, *Grace*, will also see and realize that this teaching is meant to bring you into a state of consciousness where you can live without taking thought and where everything that comes to you must come as a gift of God. As a matter of fact, it should come just a little bit before you need it and even before you know you are going to need it, since the heavenly Father knoweth what things you have need of, and it is his good pleasure to give you the kingdom.

Therefore, this is a teaching to build a state of consciousness in which you never think of a person, place or thing in this world, and yet find yourself moving harmoniously in and among and with and through persons and places and things and in "green pastures": "The Lord leadeth me . . . in green pastures . . . beside still waters. . . ."[4]

But, you see, not my conscious thinking does it, not my treatment does it–oh, no! The law of God which I am in my innermost being, that does it. And I just go along for the ride to see how beautiful the scenery is and to be grateful for all the wonderful people with whom I come in contact, for all the beautiful scenery I am permitted to see, and all the beautiful experiences that come to me.

It is developing a state of consciousness which is that of a beholder, a witness to God's work, that's all. As individuals we are spectators, watching the divine play, watching the divine flow of life, through us and in us and as us. We live and move and have our being in good. This power of good acts upon us—and really, not upon us! It really acts as us. We are it in action.

"I have overcome the world!"[5] We don't dare make a statement like that as long as we have an anxiety about anything there is between the bottom of the ocean and the top of the stars. We can't say, "I have overcome the world, but I am afraid of a bullet or an atomic bomb!" We can't even say that we have overcome the world if we fear, or believe, that death is a possibility or an inevitability! Or, that we will be any different in what the world calls death than we are this minute.

"I have overcome the world" means that one has overcome the belief of separation, of lack, of limitation, of sin, of disease, of desire, of fear, envy, hate, jealousy, malice—that is what this is to bring about. You say, "Why, that's the millennium!" Well, it is, so far as you and I are concerned; it is the millennium for you and me. For us it is the millennium because we have approached that place where death doesn't exist any more, where lack and limitation don't exist anymore, where sin and fear don't exist any more.

Now, in making this tremendous transition, it is a little bit natural that there should be an overturning in thought—a little questioning—for the simple reason that you are being roused out of your humanhood. This teaching, if it does nothing else, is certainly going to lift you forcibly out of a great degree of humanhood! It isn't going to leave you where it found you! Either you will definitely see that you have been roused out of a lethargy, or you will find yourself roused out of a mental turmoil or a life of mental pressure from demonstrating by mental means—of having to demonstrate something each day or each week or each month—health, supply, or this, that or the other thing. All of a sudden you find that your mind isn't being used anymore for any such purpose.

This, in itself, is upsetting. It is really an upsetting experience to stop thinking and just sit back and rest in God. At first it leaves you afraid. You think, "I wonder if I will wake up tomorrow if I don't go through all my lessons today!" Yes. In this work I have seen people who first gave up doing their daily lessons. Other people were compelled to give up their daily treatment or affirmation. Then they wondered if the sky would not collapse and fall down upon them for not making those affirmations and denials. It won't—there's a God! There's a God, but you know right well that not too many of us believe it. We believe that our treatment or our affirmation or our denial was the God that made everything all right. And that isn't the God at all. *I* am—and every time you say, *I* am, you are declaring the presence and the power of God in your experience.

You could go all through the balance of your career without a treatment, without a lesson, without reading a book, and find greater harmony, greater peace, greater health than you have ever known, just with the simple realization of, "Thank you, Father, I am!" *I* am! Not will be, and not shall be. *I* am! Not ought to be and not deserve to be. Just, "Thank you, Father, I am!"

In fact, if you just say, "Thank you, Father–God is," it would be just as well; just the acknowledgment of deity, just the acknowledgment of an infinite invisible presence and power which is a reality of your own being! That's all anybody ever needs. All these books we're writing and all these notes we're taking and all these talks and lectures and all the meditations, they have only one purpose: that is to bring you to the conscious realization that *I* already am!" Funny, isn't it! All these years and we're just now waking up to the fact that *I* already am!

Yes, that's the purpose of our reading. Our reading will not establish God. Our reading will not make error any less error than it is. It is already nothing. Our reading and our meditation are only for the purpose of coming into the realization that that which has been since before Abraham–and is now, and ever will be–is really and truly that life.

Now, many here are not well grounded in any metaphysical teaching and have not had the approach of the real spiritual nature and infinity of their own being. Others have gone through different approaches, thinking of themselves as humans with demonstrations to make. When you stop to think that now we are all met together in one place for one purpose–the denying of that whole humanhood we were so busy demonstrating, denying it because it's an illusion, a false sense of reality–and that we are admitting the revelation of Jesus, "Hast thou been with me so long, Phillip, and hast not known, thou seest me, thou seest the father that sent me"[6]–it is no wonder there will be questioning.

The question comes up: "Who and what is the authority for all this?" It would be easy to turn around

and say: "Well, Jesus is! Haven't you read the New
Testament?" But it would be wrong to put the responsibility on any person and way or say that any person is
authority or responsible for this. It may well be true that
there is a man of Galilee and that he gave us this teaching and its approach (and, of course, I myself, from an
inner conviction, believe very firmly that there was this
man, Jesus). But that hasn't anything to do with the
teaching. The authority for the teaching is in its results;
what it has accomplished, what it is accomplishing, for
those who live by it. In other words, "The proof of the
pudding is in the eating," not who originated the recipe.

Even though Jesus may have given (or did give) this
truth to the world, he was certainly not the originator of
it. Throughout his whole record we find credit given to
the Hebrew Prophets and the law-makers. Those who
study comparative religions or the philosophies of the
world, find every statement that Jesus made in other
forms with the same essence, back as far as a couple of
thousand years before Jesus.

So it isn't necessary to pin any authority onto a man,
or onto a woman. The authority is its demonstrability–
the authority is its usability. That's the authority for it.
The very moment you begin to take the attitude toward
life that there is a beneficent power–an all-knowing,
omnipresent, omnipotent being–and let go of your
personal effort, you find that this principle works. You
become the authority and your own demonstration.

There is a second part to this presentation I am giving
to you. I don't know of any other presentation that
makes of this a major point. This second point that I
make is not easily found in the teaching of Jesus so we
can't go back to him for authority. We can find a few

quotations of his that bear it out, but that would hardly be going to him as authority for the principle. That is what I have given you as to the nature of error.

The newest approach that you will find to this is in the teachings of Herbert Eustace. He has caught the vision that error—that which the world calls error, sin, disease and death—is not person, place or thing, and therefore, is not to be tackled from that standpoint. So that part of this teaching is quite similar to this; in many ways it parallels this.

Aside from that, I would not know where you might go in the metaphysical world to find the handling of error. You might say, "Well, perhaps it isn't important!" I am going on record to tell you that I think it is more important than knowing you are spiritual! There have been people all through the ages who knew there was a God and who knew that they were close to God, yet got nowhere with their personal demonstration of health and harmony. The entire metaphysical field is missing the boat on this point, making it necessary for new writers and new teachers to come along, until enough come along to change the whole situation that exists.

What do you think is wrong in the metaphysical field? There is something wrong. If there wasn't, the Christian Science movement with seventy years' advance and an organization that is spread worldwide, would be encompassing the world with its healings. Every metaphysician in the world would be glad to flock to it. And with Unity that began in 1894 or 1892, and with all the other metaphysical movements that began in 1890—you know, by now half this world ought to be metaphysicians! If you think of them with seventy-five years head start and our group here of two weeks, can you imagine what ought to be happening in all the rest of them? They ought to have audiences of thousands! And they would have, if they were bringing out what you originally went to them for: your health, your peace of mind, your well being.

Now, there are lots of people who are finding in Christian Science, in Unity and in New Thought, and all these various teachings, the very things they need. There is no question about that. But that none of these are meeting it on the full basis which they should be meeting it, shows that there is something lacking. There is nothing lacking with their integrity; there is nothing lacking with their love of mankind. Anybody in this work at all has got to love mankind and love them lots to be in it. The real workers in the Christian Science field, the real workers in the Unity field, the real workers in the New Thought field, are the finest people in the world and the most sincere. They are, do not fool yourself about that.

There is something beyond that. That something comes down to one single point: the healings aren't there that should be there and there must be a reason for it. Until you put your finger on that reason, we'll keep on the same way we have for the last twenty-five years. There will be a hundred of us coming to metaphysics and ten of us having our needs met. The other ninety will be struggling and struggling and going from practitioner to practitioner and from teacher to teacher and from book to book.

No, there is something wrong. Too many people in the metaphysical world are still trying to reform and heal men and women—*and* remove disease. That's where the trouble comes in. There can't be a God and a sin and a disease. Anyone who thinks so, is back in the old theological world where they not only have God but even go to church and pray to God to heal their disease. We don't do that in metaphysics–not in any branch of metaphysics that really knows what it's about. You come to realize that you are not a human being–that God is the life of you, and the mind of you is eternal. All that appears as sin and disease is just this vast universal belief that keeps hammering against your thought and which you first accept in and then try to get rid of.

The secret of harmony–whether in health or wealth– is the impersonalization of good and the impersonalization of evil. Take my word for it, that's the truth! And don't try to evade this thing by saying, "Oh, we're not concerned with healing anybody. We aren't interested in healing anybody!" You bet we are! We're very much interested in it; otherwise, we should be out in some other type of work. This work is dedicated to the purpose of bringing out harmony in the mind and body and pocketbook of individuals. We can go all the way back to Jesus for this. John, in prison, gets a little frightened that maybe Jesus isn't all he thought he was, and he sends word and asks him, "'Art thou he that should come?'[7] Are you this Christ? Are you this one we've been expecting?" Jesus did not say, "Yes, I am," and he didn't show him his certificate from the School of Rabbis, either. But he did say, "Go and show John what things ye have seen: the sick are healed, the dead are raised, and to the poor, the Gospel is preached."[8]

Now, if there is any other proof of the rightness of spiritual truth, if there is any other measuring rod, you have to get outside of the kingdom of Christianity for it. In Christianity, there is only one measuring rod: "Go

and show John. . . ." Through this truth the sick are
healed. So don't turn around and say, "Oh, we don't
care about healing!" Jesus never got so superior that he
did not heal the multitudes and supply them, too, with
fishes and bread. He didn't get above them; he stayed
right there where they were and met their needs on their
level. He stopped the storm at sea.

As I said, it does not make any difference whether a
man named Jesus did this or the power of Christ did,
because we have seen it operate in these modern days.
We've seen this Christ actually stop storms at sea (or
storms for airplanes up in the air, or stop fogs for those
out in buses). We have seen it too many times to doubt
that the Christ meets your problem right where you are.
It does it, not by taking thought for your life, but because
it is the divine Comforter—the infinite presence within
your own consciousness.

In approaching this healing work, you must make the
acknowledgment to yourself that while healing isn't the
end and object—which is to bring people to spiritual
living—the proof that this is the way to spiritual living is
in the healing that it brings in lives. The end and object
we know and accept, but don't shirk the healings. Every
time you are called upon, do all that your highest sense
can bring out to bring it about. This has nothing to do
with whether a person is deserving of the healing or not.
It hasn't anything to do with whether you like the person
or whether you don't or whether he is living a life you
like or don't like. If he comes to you for healing, you do
the utmost you can. Use the highest understanding you
have to bring it about.

That does not mean to let some people use up your
time and energy in sitting around arguing this proof with

you, or wanting to refute it or combat it. They deserve to be healed too, and they'll get over that trait. But take them as absent patients; do your work for them absently. Those to whom you give your time (and permit to take up your time), are those you feel are on this path because they want to know the truth of being—they are hungry for it. If you have the bread and the water and the wine to give them, it doesn't make any difference whether you sit up all night or get up to go calling in the middle of the night, or what you do. That's what you are here for; that's your purpose of being in this work.

For those who merely want to sit around and argue some philosophy of life or prove how wrong you might be, don't let them take up your time. If they want help for healing or for supply, let them phone you and ask for help and give them the help absently. Give your time and attention to those who humbly say, "Give me something to drink . . . give me this pearl of great price." Then give it to them!

I said that in approaching this healing work we were going to have questions and answers. I've been doing the questioning and the answering so far! Remember that the first half of our presentation was right identification—realizing your spiritual identity and the infinity of your own being—and the second half has to do with the impersonalization of error; not pinning the error on a person and then trying to get rid of it there. Remember that it is somebody hypnotized, asking you to remove their "white poodle." Don't be in a hurry to remove their white poodle because that will prove you are hypnotized too, and it would be the blind leading the blind. The way you can help is by keeping yourself un-hypnotized and realizing, "Thank you, Father, that I know there is no poodle there to be removed and the Father within doeth the work."

An illustration came to me today which originally came from ancient scripture or ancient literature, and that is this: If you were in a little boat on a river and another little boat came along with no one in it and it bumped into you, you would not get mad about it. You would realize that an accident had happened and you would do something about adjusting it. That is all there would be to it. But—suppose that boat came along with a man in it. Then you'd get mad because he bumped into you and nearly hurt you and wasted your time. There is just the point we are making! A person comes and says, "I am sick," and we immediately go back to review it, to do something about the person. Actually, there isn't any person at all; there is an empty boat. The error isn't a person at all; it's just a little accident—a little belief. It is impersonal error, not personal at all.

So, when this little boat starts coming to you, don't get mad at it. Just make a little adjustment in your realization that it is nothing. So when a person says, "I'm sick or I'm sinning or I fear," try to visualize that empty boat. There isn't any person there so there is no purpose in answering back to a person, or trying to correct him or heal him or bawl him out. Do you see what I mean?

Do not get hypnotized with the appearance of a white poodle—there isn't any! Don't get hypnotized with an appearance called a disease or a sin—there isn't any! It's an appearance coming to you. You've got to learn to be quick to realize that it is only an appearance and you can't do anything to that non-existent white poodle or the man who isn't in the boat!

The more quickly you learn to treat every problem that comes at you in that way, the better healing work you will do. One of the reasons more isn't being done in the metaphysical field, is that too much attention is being paid to heal (or change, or correct, or improve) people or get rid of sin, or get rid of disease. The field is mesmerized with the appearance instead of being practitioners who aren't fooled by the appearance.

Have no more of sending thoughts out to people—all you are doing is manipulating the human mind. Don't do it. If you have to treat, treat yourself. Treat yourself against the belief that God ever created a mortal anywhere on earth to be sick or sinful. If God didn't create a mortal, there are no mortals. Then that whole picture is like our white poodle—illusion.

Unless you pay attention to both of these parts of this particular unfoldment, you are not working along the line of this teaching. Don't try to parallel this with any other. Try to take this, as it is of itself, and either make it work, or try hard to make it work until you find you can't. Then say, "Well, I guess I was on the wrong track, or it wasn't for me." But don't try to work it in; don't try to see how it fits in with what you thought Christian Science was, or Unity was, or New Thought was.

Don't do it because I am telling you frankly that it won't work. There are too many things in all of those teachings that are not included in this at all and would only befog the issue. There are only two parts to this presentation that I am giving you: one is the infinite nature of your own being as the very I Am of God; the other part is the absolute nothingness of sin, disease and death, and your ability to impersonalize them—to say they don't exist as persons, conditions or places; to say it's only illusion or suggestion. In proportion as you learn only those two simple little things, you'll find it will work for you. All the rest, so far as this presentation is concerned, is left out.

Now, we take full responsibility in this work when calls come for help. We don't assume that the patient isn't doing something that he should be doing, or isn't grateful, or isn't sincere. We do our best. If he is not, he is going to pay his own penalty in whatever way it is. Let us be grateful; let us be sincere and not worry about the patient. He may get the healing, you know, in spite of all his wrong doing or wrong thinking, according to our standards. So let us not be critical of him. Let us assume the responsibility and if we don't make the grade, if we don't heal all of our cases, then just let's be frank enough to acknowledge, "Well, I guess I didn't rise high enough, that's all! If I had risen higher in consciousness, it would have been met."

Now, after eighteen years, I can tell you that this is true. There isn't a single case in the world that can't be met. If the other practitioner didn't meet it, it came to me. If I didn't meet it, and if it went to enough other practitioners, sooner or later it found one that met it! There is no excuse for lost cases. The only thing is, you and I can't meet every case that comes to us. Some of them demand a little more in some respects than we happen to have at that moment. That doesn't mean it is incurable or that it can't be met—it means that on a particular day we failed to meet that particular case. It doesn't mean that you and I won't meet another or a worse one tomorrow; it does mean we didn't rise high enough to meet that one.

Be willing, then, if you don't meet it, for the patient to go on and find someone else. That someone will be found who will meet it for him. So, don't, please, ever believe that there is such a thing as a case that can't be met. And don't accept any fears about those cases that come to you.

If you can see the rightness of those two points: "'I and the Father are one; all that the Father hath is mine!'[9] . . . I include all of the qualities and the activities of the Godhead . . . I am the embodiment of all that the Father is . . . "—and not because I deserve it! No. It is mine by grace; it is the gift of God to God's own creation.

As a matter of fact, it is cheering to know that even God can't take it away from you—God is all power, but not that powerful! He can't take your good away from you, because he would be taking it away from his own self. We are not two—we are one. If I were to be deprived of a single bit of good on earth, God would be depriving himself and that is manifestly impossible. "I and the Father are one. . . . All that the Father hath is mine . . ."—and it isn't by virtue of any human goodness, it is by divine right. "Ye are joint heirs with Christ in God to all the heavenly riches. . . .[10] Son, all that I have is thine. . . . [11] Lo, I am with you always until the end of the world. . . . [12] The flames will not kindle upon you; the waters will not drown you. . . ."[13] Those are all divine promises. To whom? To you. To me. And they don't say a single word about there being any price for it. They don't say anything about having to sacrifice or take communion or do anything else in the world. It is already ours just by virtue of divine grace.

Being a good human will not bring us these spiritual blessings. The realization of spiritual blessing will make of us good humans—that is the mystery of Godliness. All the human good you can do in the world won't earn you one blessing, but God's grace will make of you the finest kind of human in the world.

So try, please, in the remaining week that we are together, not to see this in connection with your past experiences. One of the greatest difficulties that we have in this work is the clearing out of our previous beliefs about metaphysical practice and metaphysical truths. One of the greatest problems that we have is to see that many of our former practices and beliefs were founded on superstition, on personal loyalty, on personal conviction, rather than on the divine truth of being.

Now, let's begin those questions . . .

~ 10 ~

QUESTIONS AND ANSWERS

Question: *Is there any way of judging when to take a case or when to have a person go to someone else?*

Answer: From the very moment that you take hold of a case, something begins to happen. Within twenty-four hours, you know, and the patient knows, whether he feels something at work. If he doesn't, and he has any urge at all, let him go. Or, if you yourself can see that within a day or two or three there is a sign he would like to make a change, then encourage it. The wisest thing in the world is never to believe that a patient belongs to you; in other words, that you have "a patient."

No patient is mine (beyond the call that he just made). He is free to go to anybody else he wants with no feelings on my part. I don't believe that there is any such thing as a personal relationship between practitioner and patient. A person who may be a patient this minute and asks for help doesn't even have to come back and explain tomorrow that he wants another practitioner. He is not obligated to me one moment beyond the minute he asked for treatment. After that, he is through. If he comes back the next day or that night, he is doing that of his own accord but I have no hold on him and want none. Never.

Sometimes I have had cases that don't seem to respond right away, but the patient says, "I want you to go on with the work." Well, that's all right. You can be sure he is feeling something in there or he would not want you to be going on with the work. It may not yet be the healing, but there is something there that makes the patient say, "No, I want you." There is some bond. As long as he wants you, you keep right on. But at the first sign that you are not registering, that you are not "getting there," and he is realizing it, let him know he is released and free and that he is not to feel any attachment or anything else in the way of having to keep on with you. In this work, it's all by feel, nothing else.

Question: *How far do you go with patients if they want materia medica help or want to resort to medicine?*

Answer: That is a question that almost has to be answered by the case at the time. For instance, my background being what it is, I naturally have no belief that we should mix medicine and metaphysics. On the other hand it is apparent that we are not meeting every situation. For instance, just see how many of us are wearing glasses, which is a resort to materia medica. The only reason we are doing this is to suffer it to be so now. It is probably better to wear glasses, if blind, until we make the demonstration; even though we are wearing the glasses, we should not be satisfied to rest back in that. We should always be continuing to get ourselves free. In the same way, there are people who, in their initial stages of coming to metaphysics out of materia medica, may be depending on digitalis or on something that, according to materia medica, "is keeping them alive." Or they may be taking sleeping powders, something of that kind.

If they are youngsters in the work, my angle is not to bother them at all, but to do my work and to free them from it. But if I don't free them very quickly and I see they are going to keep clinging and clinging and clinging then I let them go, because I will not accept the fact that we can cooperate with materia medica and I will not go on with such a case.

Now, if a person comes along who, according to medical belief, has a cancer and it's getting worse, or something of that kind and something that means surgery or death—or where there may be a broken bone and he or she wants it set—to my mind it is far better to resort to surgery and get it over with and get back on the path, than to let themselves just cry out, saying, "I'd rather die than have surgery!"

Every time you go back to materia medica you are failing in your demonstration. Just as I said before, when I don't meet a case, I'm frank to acknowledge that I did not in that particular case rise high enough—no alibis about it. Jesus would have met it. That proves that anyone with the fullness of the Christ-mind would have met it. Therefore with me it's just a question of admitting, "Well, I didn't rise high enough! I'm going to keep on in this work and try to do better next time." So, if someone comes along and the fear is so great that he wants surgery, or as often happens, he or she may not want it but has a wife or a husband or a mother or a son or a daughter, who says, "No, we're not going to let you take this risk—you've got to have medicine," they need your help more than ever.

If someone that you know in this work has made a failure of it and has to go to the hospital, stand by them.

Your metaphysical work may pull him through where the hospital or the surgery won't. Do you see what I mean? Never let go of a person. Always remember this–again Jesus is my authority–"Do unto others as you would have others do unto you."[1] If you yourself got to the point where you just couldn't make the grade and felt you had to go to the hospital, would you really and truly want your practitioner to say, "I won't give you any help"? Of course you wouldn't.

Well, suppose someone we know falls from grace and steals something and gets arrested. What are you going to do? Say, "Ho, ho! I'll have nothing to do with you!" No! That's the time he needs you more than ever. Jesus said, "When I was in prison you comforted me; when I was sick you came to me."[2] That is when he needs it the most, when he is in the deepest trouble.

The only line I draw is where people become absolutely chronic materia medica. Then I just can't do it. If people are chronically taking sleeping powders and chronically taking cathartics and all this business, I just don't want it. They are not on this path; they are seeking only the loaves and fishes. Remember, again, they came to Jesus; he had just fed them with the bread and the fishes and they came the next day looking again. He said, "What are you looking for? Not the truth. You saw the miracle of the loaves and fishes and you want some more of that."

We are not here to cater to people who want to try a little of both, who want the easy way. But for those who are beginning, stand by and have patience with them until the demonstration comes of their freedom from those things. Or if any of us get into a jam like that, stick to us. After all, it isn't a crime or a horrible failure to fall down on one of these demonstrations. It's just one of those things that happen. What we are here to do is start over again! Lots of us get left back a grade and have to repeat the work. That's what happens right here. We go along and think we are making marvelous demonstrations, getting to the top as metaphysicians, then all of a sudden something comes along and there are our clay feet. Right then is when we need our metaphysical friends the most.

So that's my attitude. Don't cater to the medical thought and don't string along with people who are trying to benefit continuously by both. But on the other hand, don't throw any one out because he is failing in a demonstration; rather stand by and help him get back on this path. In other words, love is the principle of this work!

Question: *If God is mind why is his activity not mental?*

Answer: Well, the question really is, "Is God mind?"

Question: *Well—consciousness?*

Answer: Ah! If you take consciousness you are not taking a mental activity. The mental activity is a reasoning activity and a thinking activity. Consciousness does not reason or think. It just becomes aware. For instance, if I see you there, I am not thinking and I am not reasoning—I am aware that you are there—that's all. Now, two times two are four. God, infinite consciousness—even what we call divine mind—doesn't think that and doesn't have a mental process for arriving at it. It is just a state of is—two times two are four. Now, mind does not

make it so. There was no time when it was other than
that; there was no time in creation when two times two
became four. Therefore, there is no process of making
them four and therefore, there was no mental activity.
The only mental activity was the one of awareness. Two
times two always existed as four but mental activity
consisted of being aware of it. Do you follow that?

When I said we are not working on the mental plane,
what I meant was that the only activity of our mind is
one of awareness. We become aware that you are
spiritual—that you are the divine being—that sin, disease
and death are illusions, just nothingness or mesmeric
suggestion. But we do not go through any mental
process to make it so. We don't indulge in any kind of
mental process with the idea of making a sick man well
or a poor man rich or an unemployed man employed. If
we have any process, it is only the process of awareness;
it is only the process of becoming aware of that which
already divinely is, and, I might add, it isn't a humanly
mental process.

You can't look at a sick person and mentally say,
"You are well." That's hypocrisy and ignorance and is
really a lie. It is only with your inner spiritual discern-
ment that you can look through the human appearance
and see the divinely real which underlies that appearance. So it isn't even a humanly mental process to
become aware of perfection. Our work is becoming
aware of perfection. But you can't do it humanly with
your human mind, because nothing that your human
mind will ever know will be perfect—not even humanly
perfect. It is only when the human mind isn't working,
when in the very stillness of your innermost being, when
your soul senses are aroused—when your spiritual

awareness is aroused–that you can behold the perfect man.

That is why it is not a mental process. None of my thinking will add health to you. Again we go back to Jesus, "Who by taking thought can add a cubit to his stature?"[3] Who by taking thought can make a white hair black? "Take no thought for your life. . . ."[4] In other words, the humanly mental process has nothing to do with spiritual truth. And that, friends, is really the crux of this whole presentation I am giving you. The human mental action has nothing to do with this particular approach; no amount of knowing the truth is going to help you, no amount of declaring the truth. No amount of any human mental process enters into this presentation. It is purely through the development of your spiritual consciousness. It is through the development of the soul sense. When you are in meditation–giving a treatment as we call it–when you are still, sitting back with that listening ear, this inner thing comes to life and it shows you, inwardly, spiritual perfection. And that, outwardly, becomes interpreted as a healthy or sane or wealthy human being.

You see, right there is the meat of my whole presentation–that we are not indulging any mental processes for self-improvement. That is where we get away from the entire metaphysical field. It is a question of developing your spiritual sense so that ultimately you get to where Jesus was when he could look at the cripple and say, "Pick up thy bed and walk!"[5]

What do you think would enable a man to say that? Is there any mental process you can discover that would instantaneously raise up a crippled man so he could walk? No. If it weren't the very divine fire within, if it weren't the very spirit of God, well, he couldn't do that. You might sit down and give the man a year's treatment and gradually turn him from a cripple into a healthy man by mental manipulation and by pounding and pounding and pounding. But you could not instantaneously do that. That is the fire of God in you which does it.

That's the point that we make here. We must make love the dominating influence in our experience. We must make all of the divine qualities of the Christ active in us. We must give up all personal desires, hate, envy, criticism, condemnation; we can't indulge those human qualities. We must not fear, for then we are just missing the opportunity to bring forth the divine qualities of Christ. Why go around indulging these human things at the expense of cheating ourselves from having the mind that was in Christ Jesus?

When you have the mind that was in Christ Jesus, you don't have to do any reasoning or thinking with it. It is not a reasoning process, it is not a thinking process, it is not even an improving process. It is just looking out and saying, "Why, pick up your bed and walk!" You might add, "What's to hinder you? Is there any power apart from God?" Now, you and I could sit here and say, "There's no power apart from God. . . ." We could say it and say it and say it and nothing would happen. But as a matter of fact, there is no power apart from God and if we could just get the spiritual feel of that, we'd all go out on air.

It was brought out before, that a teacher can just sit and talk these truths from now until doomsday and not bring out spirituality in his or her class or congregation. It is like ministers in the pulpit who preach the most wonderful sermons and yet the people in their audiences go on being the same kind of human beings year in and year out, with just as many sicknesses, just as many crimes, just as much cheating in business, just as much cheating in politics. Why aren't the congregations in these churches all spiritually improved? For the simple reason that they are getting the letter of truth and they many times are getting it from a very good human up there, too. But that person or minister hasn't developed the Christ-consciousness, the spiritual sense.

The thing is not to criticize the human faults, but to lift them up to where they aren't human any more! You can't do that with human reason. You can't tell a person not to lie or cheat. You can tell them all you want, perhaps, and probably have, but it doesn't do any good. The only thing that does the work is your touching them through the spirit. You must attain to such a degree of spirituality that when you meet a sinner, he loses all desire to sin. That is when you are functioning as a spiritual teacher; that is our part of the work. It isn't really teaching classes a lot of new truths and a lot of new mental processes; it is to give the age-old truth that has been tried and found—wonderful! Found so by Elisha and Elijah and Isaiah and Jesus and John.

The simple old truths can all be summed up in less than one thousand words and then, through developing our own spiritual qualities, we bring out spirituality in those we meet.

Question: *Why did God take us down into Egypt—so called?*

Answer: The question is why does God take Egypt to bring us to this. Knowing that God isn't a person sitting around manipulating the world, we know that he is our very own consciousness. God is forever imparting its truth and its guidance to us, but we are not always listening. So, we take a round-about way. It isn't God that is sending us round-about, it is we who are doing it. God is always right there imparting his impulses until ultimately we get back.

Then we say, "My very going down into Egypt was responsible for my later becoming prince of this country. In other words, had I not had that experience, I would not have learned the lesson involved and heard the voice and come back!" It isn't really that there was a God who made the brothers sell Joseph, but there was undoubtedly a state of consciousness of Joseph which meant that ultimately he was to be the King's right-hand man. He was fitted for it—that was his divine consciousness—and in some way he had to be brought to the proper place. Even though he himself could not come gradually to it, it was always there pulling and pulling, until ultimately he did land there.

You may remember this sentence in Mrs. Eddy's writings, "We come through suffering or science . . ." which means we come through suffering or knowledge—understanding. She did not necessarily mean you come through Christian Science. Well, now, that's true. You could take all that I have said here in these two weeks and immediately start to put it into practice and gradually, through that understanding, come out into perfect harmony. Or, you can say, "Yes, I'll do as much of it as I can, but I must indulge this bit of humanhood today, or I must indulge that." Now, you get there, ultimately, but you'll come with a lot of suffering. And that's the way it is with all of us.

For instance, we could take a stand right now that, "All that the Father hath is mine"[6] and that "Never again do I have to take thought for supply." We could take that stand right now and demonstrate it! But most of us won't. Most of us are going to still be a little bit worried about next month's bills and we are going to take thought about this or that or the other thing; and to the degree that we take thought, we are violating our understanding, aren't we? To that degree, then, there will have been a period of suffering, though we do ultimately get there, and that's what happened to Joseph. Had he been attuned, he could just as well have said, "I think I'll move to Egypt," but he didn't. He thought that he was going to stay with his father and his brethren, so he had to get picked up and kicked into Egypt!

When he was in the household, he could just as well have said to himself, "I am going to live as pure, spiritual being and never let mortality enter my thought," but he didn't. The chances are that he liked Potiphar's wife and thought, "Well, what's the harm?" He had to go down into prison and there learn that the indulgence of any form of mortality has no place in a spiritual being's experience. So when he was in prison, all he had time for was to think, and that's when he finally came to the realization, "Well, if I'm spiritual, I guess I'd better act like it!" It does take the very depths, sometimes, of human experience to bring us to an awareness where we are willing to let the spiritual light gleam.

Question: *Mr. Goldsmith, I'd like to ask if you can explain an experience that came to me a couple of years ago. I have been wondering about it. I was asked to go to a seminary where there* *was a very sick man. When I got there, I saw a man lying in bed, perfectly motionless. I did not know why I did it, but I began with the first chapter of Genesis and explained to him the perfection of God's creation. Then I went on with the other chapters in a way I had never done before, and quickly showed him that was man's misapprehension of what God had done. I was there just three-quarters of an hour. Without asking any questions I got up and said, "Can you accept what I have said?" He said, "Yes, I can. I have often pondered the problem of good and evil and have written along that line." The man who had taken me there said, "Work for him a couple of days." I don't remember how I worked or anything else, but the man who had come for me visited me with his wife and spent the evening with me. I said, "I never thought to ask you what was the matter with that man, but from his state of immobility I got the sense that it was something to do with his getting about." The man laughed. "He was going to the hospital the next day. The doctor said he was paralyzed and might never walk again."*

Answer: It had to do with your receptivity to truth, which is the highest form of metaphysical treatment or work there is. When we start working mentally and then call it God-healing, it is just ludicrous. But when we get a state of receptivity so that when any case comes this ear is open and the impartation comes like a flash, telling you how to work or what to work or what truth to reveal, then you can call it God-healing.

Question: *Then you think that was God-healing?*

Answer: There is no question about it, because it came to you without any thought process; it was not conscious thinking. It was a state of receptivity which revealed that truth to you. I call that being "divinely led." It did not consist in sitting down and giving a treatment against a disease or a condition. I don't believe in those treatments. Turn to God and let God show you! Ask, "What is the need of this moment?"

Can you imagine what a man wrongly imprisoned would feel if I said, "There is no injustice, man is perfect?" He would throw the words back at me. But the minute one is led to show him, say, the Book of Genesis, then he could commence to get the idea of what the spiritual sense of forgiveness is. Forgiveness does not mean saying to Adolph Hitler, "Go on! What you did was perfectly all right!" It isn't that at all. The higher sense of forgiveness is looking through the human activity and seeing that there, at the center of his being, sits God, which at the moment he is misinterpreting.

So I say this: In all cases of treatment—and certainly I religiously follow this—never do I permit myself to think a thought, even to make a denial or to affirm a truth or to think a thought. I sit down when necessary and take the attitude, "Speak, Father, for thy servant heareth. . . .[7] I will listen for thy voice. . . . Be still and know that I am God. . . .[8] Let the imparting voice come in."

Take the attitude that this is God's universe and let God do something about it. Let us be a witness to watching God in action, then usually we are led to say the right thing or think the right thing or to do the right thing. That's how all these "Letters" came to be in existence that have been out these many years. Whenever I had letters from people out of town asking for help, no matter what the problem was, I would sit down and turn within and let the Father speak. Then I would write a letter on the problem. Because we were dealing mostly with Christian Science, I might take a quotation either from *Science and Health* or from one of Mrs. Eddy's writings, and then build the letter around it. But I always exemplified a particular point of what we call truth.

To take the attitude that I can give a treatment–No! You see what I mean? That is the approach to this thing. The more you live with this receptivity, the more you live and develop this receptive ear, the more the divine voice will speak to you at every point and at every call. Sometimes, too, it does not come in words.

Jesus' words are literally true when he said, "I can of my own self do nothing.[9] When I speak of myself, I speak a lie.[10] My doctrine is not mine. . . . "[11] That is our attitude and I don't care whether Jesus said it or not. It's true! You cannot as a human being ever have enough power even to meet a simple cold. It has to be that divine impulse. It has to be that thing we call God or the Christ.

The only way you can bring that to bear on a case is when you set your human thinking aside and sit there and become the vehicle for the activity of the Christ. Then the right words come, the right thoughts come, or the right feeling comes. I have seen that with so many different kinds of cases that if I could just be receptive enough, the answer would come on the first visit; we'd have instantaneous results. But in other cases one has to make a second or a third visit–sometimes it takes two years or three years. It all depends on the situation. I have had cases that have been long-drawn out and which took lots of patience and lots of work. I have had cases where, in the beginning, I have had as many as ten, fifteen and twenty telephone calls in a twenty-four hour period–incessant calls. Then I would watch them gradually going down to ten and five and two, and then one every other day, and so on.

The process is always the same. Always let Christ do the work; let this inner infinite thing we call the Christ–the Comforter, the Holy Spirit, the spirit of truth–let it do the work. Let us not try to make of ourselves mental workers with mental processes or treatments. While these probably do work for some people and do work on certain levels of thought, it is not the approach for us. Any of the things I have said tonight should be taken in no spirit of criticism or condemnation or judgment. It is to be taken from the viewpoint that those activities have nothing to do with this particular approach of ours. And I do believe this approach will give you the greatest returns. The work has spread the way it has just because the results do come and they come because of this infinite presence which dispels the illusion.

Question: *Can we all develop this receptivity?*

Answer: Yes. It is a matter of development. We can all develop it. It is a matter of desire and of faithfulness to it. It is, though, a major work. We must devote our lives to it–give up everything of a distracting nature, every-thing of a material nature, everything of an interfering nature and put our whole life into this. This is not something that can be accomplished by the simple desire to do it. Don't expect this to be just a course of lectures where you sit back and do nothing. The intent of these classes is to shake you from head to foot, out of

your human peace into an activity which makes that
shake-up welcome. If it does that, then from then on, it
is really work!

It means giving up loads of time and maybe money.
It is really something that you put everything into if it is
to be worth anything. This is actually the Christ–living
the spiritual life. It is getting to that place where "Christ
liveth in me."[12] If that is desirable to you, you've got to
work for it; going from a human being to a spiritual
being is not done in one bound. Even Saul of Tarsus had
sought the truth for years and years and years under a
Hebrew teacher. He was going in the wrong direction,
but his heart was right; he was seeking God. No matter
how erroneously he made his way, his purpose was
truth, and ultimately all of that was wiped away from
him in one blinding flash and he saw the Christ!

So with us. It does not matter what path we have
been on, and it doesn't make any difference what we do
from now on. What really counts is the degree of
earnestness with which we are seeking truth. Can we
agree that we are no longer seeking a demonstration of
things but are seeking the consciousness of the presence
of God and a willingness to let the things be added?

In that earnestness we will develop. That is why I
have said there are three very necessary things on this
path. The first is a teacher who has caught some measure of it and who can keep listening and listening and
guiding and guiding. The second is inspirational reading,
metaphysical reading, scriptural reading, but only that
which appeals to your own path and not because the
reading is good for somebody else–the reading that is
good for you. Third is taking the opportunities to gather
in groups who, like ourselves here, have not a selfish

motive. All that we come for is to hear about God—there isn't anything else. Some of us want that knowledge to become better or to get healthier or wealthier or happier, and that isn't wrong, either—that is a right desire.

The main thing is that we are here mainly for God and truth and therefore, there must be an atmosphere of purity in this room that you can find only in places like this. So every time you go to a metaphysical meeting, or to a church meeting, you are being with people whose main purpose is seeking God, no matter on which path they move. You can get a feeling of meditation and peace and the Christ in any church, and you can be happy with groups of people of any faith. The main thing is to be among people who love God and truth and are seeking it in some way. In the end, if the desire is for God, they will have God. There is no greater example of that than Saul of Tarsus who became St. Paul.

~ 11 ~

ARGUMENT OR TREATMENT

THE TEACHER SHOULD SIT AND HEAR in silence and then let the divine mind impart the truth to you, then there would be no possibility of misunderstanding. But while we are using words, these words are cloaking the real meaning. It is, therefore, necessary for the student to discern the meaning between the lines.

As you know, I don't like affirmations and denials and I disapprove of them heartily in this work. But I want to clarify that statement to this extent. Do not think that we do not use the argument in the work. I have tried to make that clear by indicating a difference between the word "treatment" and the word "prayer." Such things as affirmations are strictly out in this work. I mean by that, reciting the scientific statement of being a hundred times or twenty-five times, or the Lord's prayer ten times, or "every day prosperity is making me rich;" those things are strictly no part of this message. But argument is not out—argument is that part of this work which I call treatment. Now, you may use very little treatment most of the time and then you may find occasion to use a lot of treatment and I will illustrate each bit of that:

A call comes for help and ordinarily, in the course of the day, it gets very little in the way of treatment. I mean that usually, when the call comes over the telephone or in a letter, the state of consciousness the practitioner or teacher lives in and maintains is sufficient. Realize that this call has nothing to do with a person, it is just suggestion—that, then, seems to take care of it. Most healings are brought about through nothing more or less than some statement: "I will be with you," or "I will take care of it," or "I am standing by." It is our consciousness of truth, spoken or unspoken, which reveals the harmony of being.

Of course, the word "I" means God. You should certainly know that when you say, "I am standing by," meaning that God is standing by—then your patient is in the best hands in the world. Now, if you were just saying that as a human being, "I, Joel Goldsmith, will stand by with you," that's pretty dangerous. "I, Joel Goldsmith" can never do anything for you; "I can of my own self do nothing." And even if I were Jesus Christ, I would have to say, "I can of my own self do nothing. . . . "[1] It is the Father within me, this divinely realized state of consciousness, that doeth the work. It is the consciousness that is developed through the hours and hours and hours of study and meditation and prayer and the living-above-sense testimony.

Most of the healing work—I am speaking now for myself—is accomplished just as simply as that, at the very time of the telephone call. Incidentally, let me say right here, never tell anyone that you'll give him a treatment tonight or an hour from now! Every call for help must be met at the instant of the call. Tonight might not get here. Meet your cases and meet them—now! All you have to do is sit there and realize within your being, "Am I fooled by appearances? Do I believe there is a power apart from God? Is there more than one life? And isn't that life, God? Isn't this just the way that universal belief is coming at me and making me believe it's a person or a condition, when all the time it is hypnotism–hypnotic suggestion. It is a white poodle that doesn't exist; neither the disease nor the person exists. All that exists is the divine mind that appears as person."

You must meet these calls as they come to you. Now, let us say–and I am again illustrating from my own case–that an hour or two later, or a half hour, or twenty minutes later, or six hours later, that patient comes right back to my thought again, either without any contact from him or by his phoning again for help, or by a telegram. Again I have to meet it in some way. As long as that person or his problem keeps coming to my attention, I have to meet it in some way. Now, I can meet it in the absolute, if I am in that high state of consciousness, by realizing the One. Or, if it doesn't satisfy me that something has been done, I may have to close the door of my office and not see the next patient, sit there alone and go into meditation. I may have to reach the center of my being and call, "Father, reveal thyself! Let me feel the reality of being!" Nothing about that patient or his claim–my mind is stayed on God.

I continue in that meditation or in that silence or in pondering God, until the answer comes, until something within me responds and says, "It is done!"–not necessarily in words, but I have the feeling that it is done, or a sense of healing, or a sense of such complete freedom from the person and the problem that even if he called ten minutes later and said, "I am worried," I would pay no attention to it. I have already had my answer. It may take him ten minutes or ten hours before he realizes his healing, but I am done with him. The moment this problem has released itself within me and I am free, the healing has taken place. The person doesn't always realize it as quickly as the practitioner.

I have had the experience of having to sit up all night, meditating, pondering some statement of truth, lying down and taking a nap for fifteen or twenty minutes, getting up again, now pondering or reading or meditating for two hours, and perhaps starting all over again—until the answer came! Why is that? Well, remember how many times Jesus went away for forty days? We don't get a chance to get away for forty days, that's the reason. We can't always remain on the mountaintop. Some practitioners and some teachers have their work so organized that every week they can go away for two or three days and just sit up on the mountaintop with God. We haven't yet accomplished that.

No, it just hasn't worked on those mountaintop experiences. I have to take my mountaintop sitting in my home or office and when the world is asleep at night. That is one of the reasons that once in a while, these claims come that catch us unprepared spiritually, so that we can't catch the answer as quickly as we should. You will find that when a call comes to you after you have had days and days of good reading, or good association with some friendly associates or speakers, and you have been in high consciousness, you scarcely know whether it is a hard case or an easy one; it just melts away. But when you are in the routine of your particular work and sometimes I in mine, we are not always in that high place and for that reason, error—which is nothing—makes itself apparent to us as if it were a horrible devil. At those times we can't seem to get the feeling that it is nothing. That's when we have to stick with it. Now, if I were going to give a treatment and I am sitting here, with some case being presented to me of what seemed a serious nature, I might ponder (it would come to me) on life. I would think about life and God and of the fact that there is only one life and that life is God. Because it is, life must be eternal—must be infinite, must be omnipresent—and it must be the life of every individual so that nowhere in heaven or on earth could there be an impaired life, a diseased life, a dead life, a paralyzed life, a sinful life. I would realize surely that only a mesmeric suggestion could testify to error and this is reversed in the understanding of one mind. Thought would go from one thing to another and then finally it would die out and there would be awareness of life and God. That would be treatment or the use of argument. But I would not feel that my work were done there. At that point would begin what I call prayer. Prayer is, to me, a state of receptivity. Treatment or the argument just lifts us up, pushes us up, to where we can apprehend or catch the word of God as it comes into consciousness.

This is the third time that I have been on the platform today and I really feel about ten miles above the street! So if a call came, I don't think I would take it very seriously right now. I think I can see quite clearly that it is a piece of nonsense; but if it didn't seem that way, then I would get down and really start on treatment. Now, I would not treat the person and I wouldn't treat the condition. I would treat—me! I would treat myself! I would say, "Now, here—what is this that is touching you? This is just nothing but suggestion coming to you of a selfhood apart from God. This is nothing more than that hypnotist trying to make you believe there is a white poodle there when you know in your heart and soul there isn't. Why don't you wake up? Why should you believe—you of all people—believe there is such a thing as mortality or fear? Why should you believe there is a mind apart from God?"

I would soon see that any form of error is but the misinterpretation of good. Yes, I might do that for a little while and then I'd say, "Okay—now!" I would then sit there and I'd wait. I'd just wait until this contact comes. You know, it is just as though a little click occurred, a breath or an inhalation of breath. I just catch something like that and I have a complete sense of release. Then I can get up and go out and nothing bothers me after that. I am sure that all is well with the patient, and it usually is.

That use of the argument is legitimate and in many cases is necessary. Surely you will do more of it than I will, most of you, for the simple reason that I have been doing so much of it for eighteen years. I am almost at a place where it isn't necessary to do very much of it very often, but it is legitimate for you to do it every time any presentation of error comes to you. Then it is right for you to sit down and say, "Well, now, what is this coming at me? Is this a couple of streetcar tracks that are trying to make me believe they come together in the distance? Well, I don't have to accept that! Is there somebody telling me there is a white poodle or a black one or a pink one? I don't have to accept that. This is nothing more or less than the actual presence of God which mortal or finite sense has misinterpreted and it is up to me to reinterpret it. There is nothing but the presence of God, God infinite and all; there is nothing else!"

~ 12 ~

PRAYER AND RECEPTIVITY

NOW, THE KIND OF TREATMENT we have been talking about is legitimate, only do not stop there; do not let anybody on this path stop there because you haven't yet prayed! All you have done is give yourself a treatment. All you have done is to mentally reassure yourself that the appearances aren't real, but you haven't yet felt the Christ. And what we are interested in is Christ-healing. What we are interested in is the actual Father within—the Christ that liveth in me—the actual awareness of the presence and power of God, dispelling the illusion of sense. We are not satisfied with anything less than that!

Therefore, if you give yourself a treatment—again I repeat: never give a treatment to a patient or to a condition—give yourself a treatment to refute the appearance or the person. Then sit there in the silence with that ear of expectancy and let the answer come. Many times it will not be necessary for some of you to go that far; most of the time you will not find it necessary to use that argument. You can take a step higher than that.

That step is, when a claim of any kind presents itself to you, whether your own or someone else's, you can take the attitude of sitting down and finding the center of your own being. How you do that, of course, is something else

again. I can't give you a process. You may take the word
God or Christ or truth, and keep it in your thought and
always bring your thought back to that, keeping it up
until that awareness comes.

That is even higher than using the argument, and you
can do it if you are keeping yourself in a spiritual
condition. Don't think you can do it if you are coming
down continuously to this mortal level of living and
indulging all this sense business with horrible movies
and disgraceful novels and all that kind of stuff that the
rabble fills time and mind with. Don't think you can give
part of your time to that and at the same time be in a
state of spiritual consciousness where you won't need the
argument—it can't be done! You have got to live on
another plane than that. You can be in the business
world (I don't mean you have to leave the business
world) and still live on a spiritual level. But you cannot
fill your mind with a lot of those movies and novels and
newspaper stories and comics and still maintain a
spiritual attitude.

If you want to maintain a spiritual attitude, you must
remember, "Thou wilt keep him in perfect peace whose
mind is stayed on thee."[1] You must learn to stay as much
as you can in the atmosphere of the Christ. It is all right
to be a good citizen and decide whom you would like to
see elected and then go out and vote for him. But don't
let it trouble you if he doesn't get elected or if it looks at
the last minute as though he might be defeated. That is
not your problem at all. If you are on this path, you are
in the world but not of it. On this path it really doesn't
make any difference to you who gets elected, or if no
one gets elected. You, if you are depending on spiritual
security, on spiritual consciousness, on the presence of

God, will be safe no matter who is president or dictator; you will be safe whether there are atomic bombs or not. After all, you can't take the responsibility for the rest of the world. Even your own relatives, if they don't want to follow this path, must take the penalty of their own states of consciousness. So don't think it will do any good to worry about your parents or your children and whether they are going to be safe in heaven with you. If they are not on this path, your concern is in continuously realizing the true nature of God appearing as friend, relation or seeming enemy.

Your problem is individually—*you*. And that's not selfishness. The only reason why you are important and why it is necessary to keep this spiritual integrity is because one on this path provides safety, security and power for thousands. Your keeping your mind off of the human problems of the world and stayed on the spiritual things, may be affecting tens of thousands of people—maybe not even in the way you think, but ultimately in the right direction. No matter how far you go on this path, you may still make the wrong human judgment in outlining in any direction.

Now, my little illustration is the telephone system. If I want to reach you on the telephone, I cannot do it without first going to central; I must go to central to get connected with you. In Duke University and in many other institutions where mental practice is studied, the attempt is to get a thought across to the other person, either to project the thought to you, or to hold it for you. Really and truly, it doesn't work! With mental power I could hold a thought and if you were weak-minded enough, I could make you see it. I can hold the image of a flower in my thought and if you are just weak enough, you will soon see the image of that flower. Believe me, it is just because you are weak-minded that it happens.

You have no right to let anybody manipulate your thoughts, or to handle your thoughts, or to send thoughts to you. Never. If you are not in possession of your own mind, what good is it? If you are going to surrender your own mind, well, you would be better off surrendering your body. Jesus told you years and years ago, not to fear the man who could kill the body, but the man who could destroy your soul. And nobody can destroy it easier than by getting hold of your mind and using it for manipulation.

Now, if you were to ask me for help, I would rather have my arm cut off than to be tempted to send a thought out to you. I would not be guilty of it, but I would sit down here and I would feel this within-ness whereby I actually feel the Christ within, until I contact the central office. Then I would sit there in joy, peace and harmony until I knew it was finished. I am sure you would have had your healing, but I would just stay at the central office with God.

God, being the all-knowing mind—God being the omnipotent intelligence—knew where the call came from and it knew enough to make the contact to reach through. It did all that—I didn't! All I did was go to the center of my being, which is God. You see, it is a strange thing; it is literally true that there is only one mind. Therefore, the mind which is the mind of me is the mind of you. So when I go to the center of my own being, there aren't two people to send thoughts out one to the other. There is just one infinite person called God communing in us with his infinite children. That infinite intelligence knows just who tuned in and why and what for, and the answer goes forth.

Never do I permit myself to think of a human being. When I go to this Christ, I shut the humans out, even those who have asked for help. The mere fact that someone has asked for help or has reached out to me for help is his tuning in or his connection with the central office. My going here to God is my going to central and I suppose we meet there; that is probably what happens. Then whatever God reveals to me, God reveals to the patient. You see, I haven't had anything to do with it at all except to be the one to go to God, to the center of my being. There, perhaps, we as individuals meet and the whole work is done. But it is done by God—by divine love.

Have I made clear the difference between affirmation and denial and using the argument? Have I made it clear that using the argument is legitimate, but the purpose of it isn't to establish something out here, it is merely to establish the awareness within you of what is without here. Never forget that out here all there is, is God appearing as individual you and me. Our argument is not aimed to change or heal or improve someone out here. It is aimed to bring to our souls the assurance and awareness of the already existing perfection out here. When these people take affirmations as a rule, like Coue, "In every day and every way I am getting better," that is with the purpose of making a sick person better. When we tell a person to take this statement and repeat it a hundred times, we are doing it because we are convinced there is a sin or sickness and that much repetition is in some way going to heal it. But that is not our work.

Again, this is not to say that fine healings haven't been brought about through it, but I do not have too much confidence in the permanence of these healings because they are not always spiritual healings. I have known some of our old workers who really worked hard mentally. A healing took place all right, but because it was a mental healing, the patient might have died of the same illness a year later, or five or ten years later. So it wasn't a healing—it was one mind overpowering another temporarily. Too much of that has been going on. We are not going to indulge in this. If you are on this path, there is a reason why you are on this path and I will tell it to you.

Before we are through with this work—I don't mean this week, because it really doesn't occur that quickly—you are going to find, every single one of you, that it does not matter where you go, you will be noticed. People will see there is something about you that is different. It will be felt. It won't be you, it will be that *It*–that Christ. That is what does the work. It isn't human personality; it isn't the gift of oratory; it isn't any of these things. It is something indefinable that you become aware of, that just sort of permeates you and emanates from you and is felt. That something heals your own body and your own business. It is an attraction that attracts to you what we call supply in all its different forms.

That is why we are on this path. Remember, the work I have in mind isn't so much learning the letter of truth. Ultimately I hope you will see just two points: "I and the Father are one[2] . . . all that the Father hath is mine,"[3] and that all there is to error is that illusory sense that makes the tracks seem to come together or makes a white poodle where there isn't one. Then be finished with the letter of truth. From there on just learn to live in spiritual consciousness and to live as spiritual consciousness.

You see, there *is* an inner world. There is a world in which we commune on a different level than the outer or human level. Strangely enough, every one of you in this room has had such communion with me, or I have had such communion with you, or else you would not be here! Not one of you came here through knowing me. Not one of you came here because I am a good orator, or a good speaker. Not one of you came here because I have a reputation that you know anything about. You are practically all strangers to me. It is somewhere on an inner or spiritual level that the attraction came about that brought us here. It really was. I haven't been well enough known around here to have a reputation. Do you see what I mean? There must be something that we instinctively feel in each other that has drawn us together. That is our inner communion; it is what Jesus referred to when he said, "My sheep hear my voice."[4] It is what the Hindu means when he looks at a person and says, "You are my student." And the student looks up and says, "I have been looking for you for years!"

That is exactly it! Did you ever stop to think why so much of spiritual language is written in love language—The *Song of Solomon* and literature of that kind? It is really because this whole relationship is a relationship of love. You might say that with teacher and student it is almost love at first sight. If you don't feel it right away, you probably won't feel it later. It doesn't come through the reasoning mind. You can't select a teacher or a teaching with your reasoning mind and then find later that you really have found your teacher or your teaching. You can have teaching with a dozen teachers for reasons and then at the end say, "I really don't think that I have found my teacher."

When you have found the teacher or teaching that is really yours, it is, as I say, love at first sight. You recognize it and say, "That's it!" That is inner communion; that is communion on an inner level. It is a recognition. It is almost like looking a person in the eye and saying, "I think we are going to be friends forever!" There is an inner awareness. In many cases—and I think you have all experienced it in some degree—it is just one of those things that sometimes happens. But once you turn to this path, once this teaching becomes a part of your consciousness, you will find that there will be the entire expression of your life.

In other words, every day of the week you will find those people and circumstances and places attracted to you that you couldn't get along without, or they without you. You will find yourself drawn to those places where you can be of the greatest service at just the right moment. You are tuned in on this infinite spiritual telephone service, and it is the central that is sending out and making the contact for you. You don't make them, the central sends out and makes them for you. There is no thought of wanting anything or desiring it. This central office just hooks in and says, "Come on!" That is what I mean. When you are living this life, you always find that this central office—God—the inner consciousness of you—is really the dominating influence of your life. You don't think, you just follow the leadings that are given you to do. You follow the work. You contact just those individuals who mean everything to you.

That is really the first step in spiritual living. You might say we have taken the first step right here in being brought together on this invisible beam, this invisible inner communion. That is just the first step. From there on, as we work together, as we remain in this consciousness, you will find others being drawn to you, and your being drawn to others. You will find yourself being brought to places and places being drawn to you. You will say, "My, that's wonderful! That is just the thing I would have loved to have if I could have thought about it!" But it is always something greater than you could have thought up for yourself.

That is where we are going with this unfoldment. Really and truly our object is not just to get a little knowledge with which we can stop a few pains or change the dates on a few tombstones. That is nice work, but it really isn't nice enough for a whole lifetime of living. What we want is how to live the life that Jesus came to show us. He didn't come either, just to heal sick people or to raise the dead. That was just to be the proof that the rest of his message was true. The rest of his message was that in the spiritual kingdom we are joint heirs with Christ in God. We are of the household of God—fellow citizens with the saints.

In other words, we have an entirely different life that we live on the inner plane—a joyous life. Oh, we are part of the outer world, too, but we don't take it too seriously, because we have an inner activity. It is like being a Mason and knowing the password. Two Masons get together and they have something on the rest of the crowd.

That is like us. No matter where we would be—in any crowd, big or small—if you and I would meet, any of us, there would be a little smile passing between us. We have had a few little secrets in here that we are not telling anybody outside. We've learned a few little things about the world and about ourselves and so, no matter where we would meet–two of us or twenty-two of us–there would be just that little smile, as much as to say, "We know something, don't we?"

Yes, we do know something. We know a little bit more about the Christ. We know a little bit more about inner living. We know a little bit more about, "My kingdom is not of this world."[5] We know a lot more about how to overcome the world. And we know that in overcoming the world, all that we are doing is overcoming the beliefs that this world presents: beliefs in infection and contagion and calories and in things outside of and apart from our own being.

We're learning more than that. We are learning that Christ was not a man. Christ is a sense of divine love that flows between us and if the world would let it, would flow from man to man and woman to woman and flood the earth. And there would never be one man desiring another man's property or his wife. There would never be a country desiring a neighbor's country or their labor or their bank account. There would be a feeling flowing through the world like it is flowing through us in here. Not one of us has any thought except to be here in God's presence! And you could just as well have ten million people with the same feeling if they just could get what we are beginning to sense: an inner divine relationship–a thread running through me and all of you back to me–and in the center of it all, God, the central office, with lines running out through all of us, making us all one in Christ Jesus.

Do you see what it means to be one in Christ Jesus? Simple, isn't it? Simple. We are all one in love. We are all one in infinite intelligence. We are all one in interest. We are all one. All that I have is thine and all that you have is mine. Why? Because we all have access to the same infinity—we are all joint heirs with Christ in God. Just think of our walking out in the street, in this great city, or world, and being able to smile every time we passed a bank or a pawn-shop! Just think of the infinite supply we have pouring to us every day, as we need it.

That is what I call a fellowship in Christ, a kinship in Christ. That is why we can look each other in the eye and say, "We know a little something, don't we?" Sure. We know we don't have to go to the bank; we know we don't have to go to the pawn-shop; we know we don't even have to go to the meat store if we don't want to. "I have meat ye know not of."[6] Did you ever stop to think of that statement? Oh, there's a beauty—I wish we had a couple of hours for it! There is a beauty. I have meat ye know not of. Just think of that. The minute you have caught the tiniest vision of Christ-consciousness, you have meat, you have water, you have bread, you have supply, you have friendship, companionship, health. I have meat ye know not of; I have a substance ye know not of. Nothing outside of me can deplete me because I am being continuously filled and refilled from this infinite storehouse within. I have meat ye know not of.

It doesn't make any difference what the world is doing out there—I have something this world knows nothing of. And that presence which keeps replenishing me all the time is doing the same to all of you, is making you independent of what the outside world thinks. If we catch one tiny drop of this vision and if for any reason every one of us should wake up tomorrow morning without one single dime to our name, still we would have breakfast and lunch and the rent and everything else as long as we have received our baptism. As long as the holy Host has descended on you and you are spiritually discerning, you know, "I have meat, I have substance. . . . I am not dependent on person, place, circumstance or condition."

Just think! I am dependent on nothing but the infinite nature of my own being. Now, you may tell me, "Of course, those are beautiful words." I will tell you they are nothing more than words until you yourself catch the fire of it, until you yourself catch the feeling, "This is it!" Until it clicks within you and you feel, "Ah, I'm home!" Once that happens to you, you really can say, "I have meat the world knows nothing about." Then you can say with Jesus, "I have overcome the world,"[7] meaning "I have overcome the need for the world's sources and resources; I have overcome the need for anything from the outer realm, because I am always feeding and flowing from within. I have meat ye know not of; I have source of supply that the world knows nothing about." If you told me you haven't a cord big enough to stretch down to that well to bring up the water, I'd pour water out of my fingers for you! I mean that's the attitude, the feeling, that comes with this sense of the Christ. There is an invisible bond that exists between us because we have tasted, we have touched, at least in a measure, this inner communion.

So I, if I be lifted up, impart and bestow upon all those who are in and of my consciousness something of that infinite storehouse without depleting my own being. Jesus, with "that meat ye know not of," fed thousands and still had twelve baskets full left over that he did not need. So with us. We can keep on imparting and imparting and imparting and never, never, find ourselves run down. Now I have meat ye know not of, I have an inner presence, an inner power, that meets every situation of human experience, whether for myself or another—whether for myself or five thousand others. It isn't anything that I personally possess in the sense that I could withhold it from anybody. It isn't anything over which I have the power to say, "I can give it to you or withhold it"—nor have I the power to sell it; it isn't mine in that sense. It is mine only in the sense that this is the particular wire it is running over, if you will. I am the particular vehicle as which it is expressing. Not through which—that would make me a fountain pen with ink running through me—but *as* which this infinite presence is appearing.

As we go on, I ask you to remember this. Our relationship does not end on Friday night. We have become part of this infinite telephone system, this spiritual telephone system. We will always be one with each other and we will always feel free to call on each other, knowing that we are fellow-citizens of the household of God, fellow-citizens with the saints. We are one in Christ Jesus, and the interest of one of us is the interest of all of us. Because we have meat that the world doesn't know, and because we have it in infinite quantities and in infinite form and variety, we can share it with each other freely—there is no reason to withhold it. It is always of a holy nature in the sense that it is not personal. We are not going to make personal demands on each other and cause personal sacrifices.

All that there is, is spiritual demand, spiritual life, spiritual being. "The Father is in me and I am in the Father"[8] and you are in me and I am in you. Do you know what I mean? There is just that relationship. And always each one of us is saying, "I have meat the world knows nothing of. . . . I have an inner strength that never wavers. . . . I have life eternal. . . . I *am* life eternal. I am the very presence of God and I am blessing the world because I know that is true of every individual in the world! Whether or not they have awakened to this truth, this is the truth of their being."

Unfortunately, those who do not awaken to it, do not benefit by it, not to as great an extent. You remember the 91st Psalm: "A thousand shall fall at my right hand and ten thousand at my left hand. . . ."[9] We can't help that. If they will not awaken to their true identity, if they are still so immersed in material living, we can't help that. In every age there are but a few who catch this vision. In every age, only a few, and of those few in every age, only one or two catch enough to go right up to the heights. It is a strange thing, this work. People, driven mainly by some need, come to this Christ teaching and catch a little breath of it; it is like a breath of fresh air. They say, "This is what I have longed for always—this is where I want to go!" And they mean it. They think they do.

But this path has a habit of fulfilling our human needs very quickly. We very quickly find ourselves getting the amount of income that we think is a very generous one. We quickly—or perhaps slowly—attain a degree of health that we think is fine. And, you know, that is where we rest. We stop and pull away from this. We just rest on that level. We get so far and we stick there.

I know that to be true. With hundreds and hundreds of people with whom I have worked, hundreds and hundreds who have come a little way along the path, I have seen this one stop when he reached $50 a week, that one when he reached $150, this one when he reached $250, this one when she reached the place where her body didn't pain her any more. This one stopped when he or she found a wife or a husband or a social circle. I have seen it over and over and over. I have watched how few there were who really stuck by and watched for that "last hour," for the highest degree of unfoldment.

Now, you will have to take this on faith. There are pleasures in the spiritual realm that transcend anything there is in humanhood. There are pleasures, there are joys, there are harmonies, there are friendships that transcend any type of human relationship you have ever known. It is worthwhile to stick on this path. It is worthwhile to set your sails for uncharted seas, for the wide horizon, for the places that the average human won't ever find, won't take off for, won't give up material comforts for, won't surrender family life for. There are wonderful, wonderful places.

We do not live by bread alone. The very moment we touch this inner realm, the spiritual consciousness, we really do not live by food alone, nor by sleep alone. It doesn't mean, either, that we don't enjoy a good meal! I myself have never seen anyone who caught this vision become unbalanced. I have never seen anyone become an ascetic, or who became "odd."

To touch the spiritual presence doesn't really mean to get sanctimonious and it doesn't mean to live on a cup of milk or a bag of rice. On the contrary, I have found—not only with myself, but with many others who I know have touched a measure of this work—that they enjoy the nice things of life, the nice places of life, the nice foods. The only thing is, these don't become so important to them that they are necessary because, firstly, the awareness of the spiritual presence and power attracts the nicer things, the higher things to one and yet doesn't make one attached to them or enslaved to them. It is really a great thing to know that we do not live by bread alone, that really our inner life is fed more by our spiritual contact, by our associations with each other, let us say, than with any of the human activities of life. We can get more joy in just being together with a few people who are on the spiritual path, than we can with any number of people offering us the finest human attractions. In the same way, we can get more joy out of a few sentences or a few paragraphs or pages of inspirational writing than we can out of the world's greatest plays or dances that do not carry that inspiration. "I have meat ye know not of; we do not live by bread alone, we are fed internally." Sometimes a handshake means more to us than a whole day's automobile driving with some other people. Just passing one another on the street and waving hello can give us more of a touch of companionship when we know each other, when we know this path, than all kinds of amusements outside.

~ 13 ~

MESSIAH

FOR A FEW MINUTES I WANT TO REPEAT a little of what I talked about this afternoon. This afternoon I was in Vallejo and visited and talked to some students there. Strangely enough, I talked on a subject about which I had spoken here last week and I never said a word that I said last week. Nor did any of the thoughts go in the same direction.

I spoke on spiritual freedom and before I was through here that afternoon, the whole thing had turned itself into grace. But today the whole talk took an entirely different turn. I would like to repeat some of it now, because I think it is an important thing for us consciously to remember.

The point to which I refer is this: For centuries Jesus had been foreseen and promised as the coming Messiah. The Hebrews had been eagerly watching for his coming; they had been scanning the skies for years for this new Messiah. They were, of course, practically slaves to Caesar and they were not too happy with their church administration, which was also holding them under too tight a bond. So, with the coming of the Messiah, they thought that they would be freed of a lot of these tithes to the church and ten per cent taxes to Caesar and an

175

extra five per cent for good measure and an extra twenty per cent on holidays. That financial taxation was a pretty serious thing. You know, it was almost like taxation without representation. In addition to that, of course, they did not have too pleasant a life under Caesar.

So naturally, their expectancy was that when the Messiah came, he would certainly dethrone Caesar and make them a free people and give them their Holy Land in which to live as a free people. That probably was the uppermost thing in their minds. They would own all that territory about Palestine and the Holy Land and be enabled to live free of Rome. They would also be free of their Pharisees and Sadducees and be economically and politically and nationally a free people. Every indication is that is what they were expecting of their Messiah. You all know that he disappointed them for he did not give them one single bit of that. In answer to all the requests and all the demands ("When is this thing going to happen?"), you remember his famous answer: "My kingdom is not of this world."[1]

It wasn't in him to free the Hebrews politically or economically or nationally. That was not his mission and that was the point on which they rejected him. I am pretty sure that if Jesus had turned around and said, "Let's get up a big battle here against Caesar," no doubt they would have accepted him as their Messiah and their king. Of course that was impossible because that wasn't the nature of his mission—his ministry was a spiritual one. What he was offering them was spiritual freedom, freedom from any kind of materiality. If they had accepted this, it would have freed them from Caesar and from all the other bonds. Once a person is spiritually free, he is physically and mentally free. Their vision didn't go that far. They could not accept that type of Messiah, so they rejected him.

Our ministry today is in that same line. If we were to sit up here and say, "Let's see if we can't demonstrate a better home for you to live in and a better job and a better wife or a better husband or better children or a bigger income, or perhaps establish a colony somewhere to give you freedom from the atomic bomb, or let's have a fine army to be sure the Communists don't come in, it would not be difficult to set up that kind of Messiah.

We are in the midst of this sort of thing in this country now. It isn't difficult to set up the kind of Messiah who would promise you the moon, as long as the promise is of a material nature—like keeping sixty million people employed. We love to hear of that type of Messiah. It promises so much in a physical and in a human way, and that's the only way we seem able, on the whole, to understand.

We reject the Christ ministry which is offered us again today and is offered every day in the week just by opening our Bible and reading, "Seek ye first the kingdom of God and his rightness and all these things will be added."[2] Every time you read that, every time you open your Bible near that passage, you are being offered the same spiritual ministry that was offered two thousand years ago and which they rejected. You know how often we reject that in favor of demonstrating things or persons.

Let us watch that we are not setting our eyes on a Messiah who will give us more or better matter. In turning to the spiritual life, we are seeking this inner kingdom, this Christ within, this divine presence and guidance and spiritual freedom—meaning the freedom from material laws, from material activity, from material powers—whether the power is one of infection or contagion or of stars or anything that claims to have power. Once you have attained your Christhood, you are free. You are free from every claim of mortality. Sin, disease, lack, limitation—all these things disappear in your inner or spiritual freedom.

I want to close tonight on this note and this is the point I would like you to ponder—the question of Messiah, of what it is you are expecting and what you would like from your Messiah. Your Messiah is the Christ of your own being. The question for you to decide is whether you have arrived at that point where you can reject the temptation to demonstrate persons and things and turn right to the Christ, to the kingdom within, and attain that measure of spiritual freedom which we talked of for an hour before we got onto this subject.

On that note we will say good night.

~ 14 ~

A WORD TO THE WISE

ALL ERROR IS HYPNOTISM claiming to operate as your own thinking. As soon as you realize the error is not your thinking or that of your patient, you separate yourself from the suggestion and you become free. The act of recognizing the error—regardless of its form—as universal hypnotism or mesmeric suggestion claiming to act as your own thought or thinking, is the release. Only while the error is unrecognized as suggestion or imposed hypnotism, do you remain in the sin, disease or lack. Every claim of the body governing or controlling you, every belief of limitation, every appearance of sin or disease, lack or death, is but hypnotism claiming to act as your thinking. The realization of this truth is your remedy.

Every claim or suggestion of mortality, even good mortality, must be handled in this way. These human appearances when seen as the activity of mesmerism must now be traced back to the one mind and understood as the finite sense of mind—life and mind's formation. This reversal of the picture and reinterpretation completes the treatment and reveals divine harmony where error seemed to be.

To be a practitioner or teacher, you must in some measure have been released from this universal hypnotism so that you stand in back of this world as it were, and "see" with the un-hypnotized mind which is God. In this illumined consciousness it is evident that mesmerism, seen and recognized, is not power; it never was real power, but operated as both presence and power until detected and cast out through the realization of the Self as the all-power. Remember that hypnotism always appears as person, thing, or condition, circumstance or place.

The wise practitioner is always able to see behind the false, finite appearance because he is beholding with the unfettered mind which is God. This is summed up for us in *The Infinite Way*, as follows:

"The sense which presents pictures of discord and inharmony, disease and death, is the universal mesmerism which produces the entire dream of human existence. It must be understood that there is no more reality to harmonious human existence than to discordant world conditions. It must be realized that the entire human scene is mesmeric suggestion and we must rise above the desire for even good human conditions."

~ 15 ~

SEEK THE ANSWER WITHIN

As I TOLD YOU BEFORE, we are not here to have a good time; we are not here just to sit back and listen to a lecture on truth or to listen to a talk on truth. This is really classwork. This is really where you are supposed to go out knowing all that is to be known about the subject.

I asked you, when we began, to release me from a sense of time and you have, so if it is necessary to stay here, that is all right with me. I want you to know that, so when we are through you do not feel that you are leaving with a lot of unanswered questions. There will be some unanswered questions in your thought and that is natural, because most of the answers are going to come to you in the weeks to come through your meditation. One of the things that you will learn here is that answers come through meditation. You can take almost anything you want into meditation and get the answer.

You see, we know absolutely nothing about the meaning of the word God or Christ or truth or light or grace. What little we know we have read in dictionaries and books that men have written, and are merely faint tracings of tremendously deep subjects.

Now, the individual who has had an unfoldment or revelation on some spiritual truth may be said to know

181

that spiritual truth–at least as much as concerns that particular unfoldment or demonstration. But, when that individual comes to tell you about it, it is very apt to be secondhand except in some moments of our illumined consciousness when his impartation might reveal quite a bit to you. But to be on the safe side, let us assume for this moment that we know little or nothing about the Christ. Of course we know this much, that the Christ isn't a man. We know that the Christ isn't an historical figure; we know that the Christ wasn't born at a particular time or in a particular country or of a particular nation. We know that before Abraham was, the Christ *is*–and we know that even unto the end of the world, the Christ will be.

We know, therefore, that the Christ isn't a person but rather a presence or a spirit. Well, intellectually there isn't much more to be known about the Christ than that. It pretty nearly sums it up. But do you know that if you were going to take that explanation and try to heal somebody with it, you are very apt to fail? You would probably find it wouldn't work. Why? Because so far it is just in the realm of the intellect. It's just in the realm of a knowledge about the Christ. It is at this point that all failure in healing takes place. So much of truth is intellectually known and stated and written and affirmed yet so little has been realized.

Our metaphysical study has convinced us intellectually that this world is a spiritual one; that our bodies are spiritual, that all physical structure, good or bad, healthful or sick, is but our illusory sense of the ever present harmonious reality–and we are surprised that this knowing or affirming does not immediately produce healing. There is no change produced in the visible universe through an intellectually perceived truth. Until the truth becomes a real state of our consciousness through inner realization, no change in the outer circumstance will appear. Every question and problem of so-called human experience must be taken into the depths of consciousness until the intuitive sense has been awakened—until it has revealed to us the truth of being concerning which we heretofore have had only the illusory sense or finite concept.

Spiritual healing is an activity of consciousness, not of the intellect. It is the perception, spiritually, of that which appears to sight, materially. What appears outwardly as a physical condition, good or bad, must be reinterpreted through spiritual awareness until reality is realized in consciousness. (See chapter "The New Horizon" in *The Infinite Way*)

Now, to continue, let us take the term "the Christ" into meditation, starting with a very humble statement: "I know so little about this, Father; reveal it to me." Then you close your eyes, perhaps, and you would have the word Christ, not necessarily spelled out (you don't have to spell out the word to know that it's there), with your attention centered on the idea—the Christ. Every time your mind tries to wander off the word Christ, you gently bring it back, bring your thought back, bring your attention back, and all the time your ear is open and it is listening. While your ear is attuned, is listening, your thought—your attention—is centered up here on the Christ, and whether or not it happens the first or second or third or nineteenth time is not too important.

If you will do that, ultimately you will catch the vision of the real meaning of the Christ, a meaning that you will never be able to quite explain to anyone else. But you yourself will know it; the Christ will be an actual presence in your consciousness. It will be a power, an influence, a being, yet it will be something that you cannot define. You remember Lao-Tzu on God, when he says, "If you can define it, it isn't God." So it is with the Christ—no matter what you would say about the Christ, it wouldn't be quite it. And so the balance, the rest of the knowledge that you would need, would have to unfold from within you. The same thing is exactly true about the word, *God.* We might as well be honest here and admit that there isn't anyone in this room that knows the meaning of the word God. If you think you do, if you have any idea at all that you know what God is, think it over for quite a while and you will find that you don't know what God is.

You may have little glimpses here and there of what God is. That is all you have had and that is all you are having now. The full and complete unfoldment or revelation of what God is must come from within you. When it comes, I don't know but that you probably will ascend with Jesus out of human sight! One thing is sure: you will be living in an entirely different world than you are at this moment.

We could take another term, *light.* You know we speak of the light of the world. Jesus was that. Elijah was that. Isaiah was that. Paul was that. John was that. We have had plenty of them in later years—people who really could be called the light of the world. But what do we mean by light of the world? And here's another thing—no matter how much you know about it, there is much more to be known. And that will come to you through your meditation, through your again taking the word light or the term "light of the world" into your meditation. Turn to the Father within and ask for light on the *light.*

As you learn to develop that listening ear, you will gain the spiritual sense of the term, rather than the dictionary sense, or the sense that some metaphysical writer has given you. You have your own God-given light on the subject, *light,* so you may take any aspect—any facet—of spiritual truth. Perhaps the word soul isn't clear to you, and soul is one of the most important words in the entire dictionary.

Soul is really one of the deepest mysteries of spiritual unfoldment. Very few know what soul really means. We speak of soul as God and then we speak of your soul and my soul. But when you stop to think it over you really know that you don't know too much about soul. So you want to do some meditating and you want to take that word soul and you want to turn to the Father humbly and say, "Reveal this to me! Give me light on the soul!" Then with the listening ear, the state of receptivity, sooner or later—a day, a week, a month, a year—you will begin to receive impartations of spiritual awareness on the subject of soul.

So you see, this class isn't really going to end Friday night, is it? Except if you make it end. You see, you can end it Friday night or you can continue it on indefinitely by taking just these little gems, these little seeds, and seeing what kind of crop you have in a few weeks or a few months.

~ 16 ~

ILLUMINED CONSCIOUSNESS

AGAIN WE HAVE A TERM like Christ-consciousness, or illumined consciousness. Sometimes we wonder, "What is that thing, Christ consciousness? What is illumined consciousness?"

The consciousness that thinks of God as something separate and apart from its own being, the consciousness that has not received some training or teaching along a metaphysical line, is a very much unillumined consciousness. Let us say that is your consciousness or my consciousness before we receive any spiritual or metaphysical teaching. And now let us say that for a year or two or three we study with any of the schools of metaphysical thought. By that time we have learned of God as the reality of being, we've taken God out of the skies and identified him with us. In our unillumined state of consciousness, we thought of Jesus as Christ, but now, through illumination, we understand Christ as the spirit–of God, of the man Jesus, and of you and of me. For Jesus said that before Abraham was, he is, and that the Christ will be with you until the end of the world. So the Christ is a possibility for us.

Perhaps we have learned in the first or second or third year of metaphysical study that prayer isn't asking

God to give us sunny weather on the day we want to go picnicking and it isn't asking God to take away our sins or our diseases. Perhaps we have learned enough to know that prayer is an inner realization of our present spiritual perfection. By that time we have become an illumined consciousness up to that point; we are at least some degree of illumined consciousness.

Now, we come to this point where we learn to take into our consciousness any word or term on which we are seeking light or knowledge. We have learned now that we don't have to go to a teacher, we don't have to go to a church. All that we have to do now is to take that word or term or idea into our own consciousness and there, in a state of expectancy, wait for the light to shine on it and reveal its understanding to us. With that, we are more illumined consciousness.

You see, we are the same person; we look the same, we feel the same. Our friends may say, "Something has happened to you. You seem to have a different look in your eye or you look healthier." But that's the only change they notice. To all appearances we are the same person, but actually we are not. By now we are pretty much an illumined state of consciousness, instead of that unillumined one.

At the same time, nothing has changed in the world; it hasn't gotten to be a better world. Our sense of the world has improved. The world, to begin, was God's world and it was spiritual and it was perfect, and this illumination that has come to us doesn't improve the world at all. It improves our concept of the world, our vision of the world; we are now beginning to see it more nearly as it really is.

So that's the difference between an illumined consciousness and an unillumined consciousness. There is nothing of a mysterious nature about it; it is just your own consciousness when your own consciousness has lost some of its erroneous or orthodox religious teaching, or mental teachings, and you have come to the point where you can look out on the world and say, "Why, it's beautiful! Now I can realize that it always has been beautiful. The light is within my own vision; therefore, I am able to see the world through the lighted consciousness, through the illumined consciousness, which I now am."

That is why we have the term, "The mind that was in Christ Jesus."[1] It isn't any mind other than your own. It's in your own mind but it is your own mind after you have lost the love of error, the hate of error, and the fear of error. It is your own mind, your own consciousness, after you have learned to look out on the world and say, "There is no power outside of my own being, and because God is my own being, there is no evil power."

Well, the mind that was in Christ Jesus is now the mind of you. It isn't anything mysterious that you contact or get at-one with; it is your own mind after it has received some degree of illumination. Now, of course, this is true. The mind that was in Christ Jesus, which is the universal, spiritual mind, is already an infinite, eternal mind or consciousness and it is always there and it never becomes illumined. But as you individually receive illumination, that which we call your ignorance is dispelled and that mind which was in Christ Jesus is now your very own mind.

In the working out of a problem, you can do the same thing. Let us say a problem comes to us; it may be our own or it may be that of a patient or a friend. Anyhow, it has been brought to us for solution. It may be a problem of health. Now, you can't take the problem into your meditation but you can take the subject. You can turn in the silence within and say, "Father, this problem or person has turned to me. Let me have light." Then forget the person, forget the problem, and remember that you are only turning to the Father for light on that subject. You are not looking for a solution to the problem—there are no problems. The problem isn't out in the world; the problem is a belief in your own thoughts—let us say, the ignorance of what God is or what Christ is.

And so, you are seeking the light on this thing. You are not seeking somebody's good health, but you are seeking the truth about health, harmony, peace and joy. Remember, don't take it in as if you were going to work on a problem. The problem is presented to you, but now drop it. If you are going to close your eyes and go within, don't take the person or the problem with you. Leave that out. Just turn to the Father and say, "Give me light on this." Keep your thought on the light or the truth. Pretty soon you will feel that stirring or you will feel that click or you will get a specific answer and you will have the feeling, "It is done." Don't take your problem, don't take your ignorance into your meditation. Take the subject of truth or the light about whatever the problem may be. Then, let that light dawn.

At this point, it is almost as if we were Lake Erie. Are you all familiar with my illustration of Lake Erie? Everybody here? All right. Now, let us say that I am Niagara Falls. Up to this moment I have been believing that all there is to me is right here and I have been using it up or drawing upon it. I believed that I was living in and of and through Niagara Falls and that all there was of me was Niagara Falls; I was not aware at all of Lake Erie back of me. But through coming to this light, I now learn that Niagara Falls isn't so much of itself, but that Lake Erie is really the substance and the totality and the infinity of Niagara Falls.

I, as an individual, before this light of truth dawned, believed that the visible me is all there is to me and I drew on my own brain power; I drew on my own experience, my own education. For my strength, I drew on my muscle and on my amount of sleep and on the food that I ate. I tried not to use up more strength than I had taken in as calories and vitamins. But since I have come to this awakening, I have learned that this really isn't all of me—it is the least part of me! Back of me is an infinite ocean called God. I am in and of that tremendous ocean. As a matter of fact, I am the place where that whole ocean is going to flow through and as!

That is where we are this moment. Every time we close our eyes in meditation or every time we keep our eyes open but open this ear to hear the still small voice, to place ourselves in a state of receptivity, every time we do that we are acknowledging that there is a whole ocean of intelligence, a whole ocean of life and love and truth. We are opening our consciousness to the influx.

Why, just by opening my ear I have the whole voice of God to listen to! By just opening my consciousness, I have the whole guidance and direction and thought of God. By opening my consciousness, I have all the health and strength and longevity—immortality, eternality, peace, joy, power, dominion. Everything that belongs to God now belongs to me because I have opened my consciousness for its inflow.

Our existence must be as a state of receptivity. Our existence must be the continuous opening of consciousness for it to come through. And remember, don't limit it—don't finitize it—don't think it has to come through a perfect person or a certain book or a certain teaching. Keep your consciousness open so that it comes from God. It may appear to you as a person, or as a book—that part is all right. But on the other hand, if you are keeping your mind unlimited, if you are keeping your consciousness open, the book that meets every need for you today may be outmoded tomorrow or the next day or next year and you will be ready for a whole new book.

You would be surprised if you could see how many books I have seen unfold in this last twelve months. It is really surprising. You are going to see the same thing, because if your consciousness is open, you will never be a one-book author—one who tells all he knows in one book. But if the consciousness is open, if, you don't say, "Oh, isn't this wonderful! I guess this is the last word!" but just keep your consciousness open, there will be a new message, a new flow, continually.

This is true not only of books, but of body. There is no reason why body should ever run down. The only way it does run down is the way Niagara Falls would ultimately run down if it didn't have Lake Erie behind it. If Niagara Falls started to use up all the water in the falls and didn't draw on Lake Erie, it wouldn't last very long. If you and I start using all the knowledge in our brains and all the strength in our bodies, and even if we replaced that with calories and vitamins, we would find it wouldn't do.

There must come a time when we say, "I live not by bread alone, but by every word that proceedeth out of the mouth of God."[2] You know, the word is always proceeding out of the mouth of God, but are we listening? Or are we looking in a book and seeing what it says on page 82? Oh, yes, that's what we do over and over again. We limit ourselves to the pages of a book, even a book as big as the Bible. Why, that Bible hasn't said it all! At least it hasn't said it all in as many ways as it can be said. It never will. God being infinite, must be infinite in expression. God being eternal, must be eternally unfolding. Don't limit the infinity of God, the eternality of God or the omnipresence of God. God is infinitely, eternally with you. The only thing that can cut you off from God is closing your mind to it, closing your consciousness to it. Don't do that.

There is no such thing as a treatment understood, ever stopping. Why? A correct treatment is the word of God. If you ever hear the word of God once, rest assured that word of God will stay in action until your healing takes place, whether you receive the healing that minute, the next day or the next year. The treatment never stops.

We don't need a fresh treatment every day. The only reason we need a different treatment or a new one or a special one every day is that it wasn't actually a treatment, it was really only our very finite idea of a treatment—it was only our statement of truth. That is no treatment.

A treatment is only complete when you have finished your part of the treatment and have listened to the still small voice and received an answer. That is a full and complete treatment. That is the word of God made flesh. And, you know, the word of God must be made flesh for there is no such thing as a word of God dangling up there in the air. The word of God must be made flesh; it must dwell among us! So remember this: Once you receive an answering click, an answering sense or response to your treatment, don't worry if you never receive another treatment in your life. That treatment will operate in your consciousness until it breaks down the ignorance and reveals the illumined sense of being.

Now, as we go into the higher revelations of the Master, we will find that it isn't so necessary to voice our thoughts, to use mental might or physical power. We learn that there is within us a divine presence—an infinite power—that does much more for us than we can do for ourselves. It operates best in silence. When a practitioner can arrive in his own consciousness at a place of absolute silence, at a place when he is completely a listening ear, in just that flash—it need only last one blink of an eye—it can heal anything that ever was wrong on earth. The silence, the unexpressed thought, the real power, is in that thing we call the Christ—this tremendous energy. We see the effect of it, but never it itself. No one can ever see, hear, taste, touch or smell this infinite Christ, but we do see its effects.

Those of you who know gardens know also that you plant a seed in the ground and you cannot see any of the power that operates through that seed. You can see an effect, you can see the seed break open. You might see the inner part of the seed gradually take root and you may see something come up from the ground. All that is the effect. You never see what's doing it; it has never been seen. That is the very power that operates in the silence of the seed and it operates in the silence of our consciousness. When we attain that degree of silence, we have attained full illumination.

Now, as we learn to depend on this—let's call it infinite invisible—we find things happening in our experience that we hadn't planned that way—beautiful things, harmonious things, healthful things; and the moment we become aware of their happening, we instinctively know that it was the result of this power. We have no doubt but that these things are the result of this power, of this unseen, infinite invisible which we may call the Christ, the presence of God.

We know that is operating in us and through us and for us and at first it is a little bit difficult to find a full reliance on it. It is like that first time you try to bring out a healing without thinking. I think of all times in the world, that is the most difficult for anybody on earth. I have never been lost on the desert or stranded at sea, but I think that the first time you try to bring out a healing without thinking is worse than either of those two experiences.

We have been so accustomed to relying on some right thought or on some good thought, that the first moment we expect to see something happen without any thought, is like falling down from the top of the Empire State Building with nothing to hold us up, because there isn't a thought there to cling to. In that moment comes the first tangible proof that underneath are the everlasting arms. When you no longer have reliance on a person or on a thought, all of a sudden you begin to feel something as tangible as the everlasting arms.

Now, we think of terms like "everlasting arms" as poetry; we think of them as expressions of inspired people. But I wonder if you really know that it is an actual thing—"underneath are the everlasting arms"—that there is actually such a thing you can literally *feel*, even though you can't see it or hear it. You can actually feel it even in its invisibility.

We can become aware of it when we have begun to take our faith away from man or from thought and rely utterly on it. I suppose in Biblical language it is called faith, but in most cases faith is something of a blind sense; faith is very often a confidence in something that one does not yet know exists. So that which I am describing is not that type of thing. It is more like what you would feel if you were in the water with water-wings and then said, "I have faith." You have faith because you actually feel those wings and feel the buoyancy of them. And so you say, "I have faith."

This faith, this understanding, this confidence that I mean, comes only when you have once *felt* the everlasting arms. It isn't anything you accept before you have felt it–that would only be a faith that it can be or ought to be or might be or should be or maybe it is a reality. What I mean is that once you have had the first experience of being without the aid of person or thought and you have felt something pick you up, from then on in increasing measure you learn to lean back on that infinite invisible.

In the infinite invisible there are ties between us. There is a tie between God–the universal life and being–and its individual expression, that which we call individual man and woman. There is an invisible mind. As we become aware of that we begin to find those who belong to our spiritual demonstration, we begin to find those who are on our level of consciousness; but it goes even beyond that. We find those, even though they may never have heard of truth in any form, who may be necessary to our demonstration of the moment. In other words, there are invisible forces acting on the inner planes attracting to us those people and experiences necessary to our unfoldment. It all happens without taking thought, without planning it that way.

We contact the infinite invisible when we touch that place in our consciousness which we call God or the Christ. Even without taking any thought for tomorrow or for the things of tomorrow, we touch the center which in its infinite and invisible way is really the consciousness of all mankind. It operates on that unseen level to draw to us the harmonies of existence, whether in the form of persons, places, things, circumstances or conditions.

Now, we all know how to go about working on the visible planes. For instance, we would know how to go out and place an ad in the newspaper and so attract to ourselves those who have need of what we want to sell. We would know how to go out among our friends and tell them about something we need. We know how to live and move on this outer plane and get along fairly well.

What we are going to learn now is how to stop taking thought for the things of life, dwell on this infinite invisible, and realize that, like the central office of the telephone company, it can send out and connect us anywhere in the world. The only difference in this case is that we don't have to know the number we want; all we have to do is be in touch with God, the center of our being, and it knows and it draws and it contacts. Really, we wonder how it all came about.

If you could only see the operation of this infinite invisible! Sometimes you do see it and will see it in your meditation. Sometime you will see the whole secret of life, you will see all that underlies nature, you will see all of the forces. There are some people who are on the spiritual path and they come to a place and for some

reason it seems preferable for them to go on and to
die—pass on. However, they have been on this path, they
know better. There is just one problem they can't
surmount and they consent to going on. Now, that
person is on an ascending scale, remember, and has
been for a long time. When he passes, it is very apt to be
a release from materiality. In other words, he may have
realized that one thing, that last thing, that he couldn't
quite catch here and so be completely set free.

I had such an experience with an individual who for
twenty years or more studied metaphysics and had one
problem of health that just seemed to be more than he
could take. He couldn't meet it; it couldn't be met for
him—or wasn't. Yet here he was twenty years on the
upward path probably knowing more metaphysics than
nine out of ten, and yet not being able to quite make this
grade. Finally, he accepted this idea of passing. Within
a few hours after the passing, he caught the vision and
saw the fullness of the light and was able to give it back
to us over here. It isn't really over here or over there; it
is all here. It is only a matter of our sight and language.
In that case, then, passing is not dense materiality; it is
apt to be a progressive step forward.

When we come to this place where the infinite
invisible becomes a real part of our existence, when we
come to the place where we actually see it operate in our
experience (we don't see its operation, remember—we
see the *effect* of its operation and each day we see some
proof that something is going on in our experience
which we can't account for humanly; and of course, it is
always of a good nature), when we get to the place
where we can turn to that infinite invisible for guidance,
for direction, for advice, for health, for strength, then we

come into a state of consciousness which transcends the ordinary limited sense of time and space.

You will agree that life is immortal. You will agree that your life is eternal. That means you are agreeing that even should you, for any reason at all, experience death or passing, that would only be a momentary lapse from consciousness. You would immediately pick yourself up and go right on, because consciousness, you know, couldn't end; consciousness couldn't stop at the grave. You all have some idea of what immortality means, of what eternality means. Of course, you haven't enough knowledge of that and so that is also going to be the subject of meditation for you. You are going to learn within your own being more of immortality and eternality than you now know. You will then realize that life does not end at the grave, that life is eternal, and that life manifests itself. The word becomes flesh, eternally, in what we call our individual experiences.

Now, since that is true, life never began. Your individual life never began. You may think that it began in 1900 and something or 1890 something or 1880 something. But it never did! You may have become aware of it at that particular time and that constitutes your present experience. But as you meditate now, you are going to learn the true meaning of immortality: that long before you became consciously aware of the earth, you were living and living fruitfully and harmoniously, just as you will eternally and immortally after what is called "the passing."

You may ask, "What practical value has that?" It has a deep value and a tremendous value in that it explains to us much of the human experience through which we are passing. It reveals to us the spiritual laws that govern human experience, laws which did not begin to operate for us on what we call our birthday and laws which we will learn to have confidence in as operating in our experience should we ever consent to the experience of passing–that comes under the heading of pre-existence.

You see, if our life work had only to do with learning a little system of healing people, of postponing the date on their tombstones, none of this would be of too much importance. We would just busy ourselves with learning how to give treatments and bring out a few healings. Actually, those who have come to this room at this particular moment have shown that they have already begun to leave the state of consciousness where all their attention is concerned with whether they have a few more dollars or a few less, or whether they have a few days more or less of pain. Actually their interest is in the laws of God, the laws of the spirit, the laws of soul. So, in order fully to understand these laws we have to begin with the understanding that they never began and they will never end and because we are these laws, because we are the very activity and presentation of these laws, we have never begun and we will never end. Through that understanding we will find our rightful, spiritual place.

That is where we come into that infinite invisible system of wires whereby we draw to each other all the experiences and persons and books and understanding and knowledge necessary to our unfoldment. Now for our human unfoldment we would look into human ways, but because our unfoldment from now on will be spiritual–even though it appears outwardly as human–we will have to find the answer to it in spiritual law.

The only reason I bring up immortality and pre-existence is that when you go into your meditation you are not limiting yourself to something that you already understand humanly. Actually cut loose, turn within and ask for a revelation of eternal good, of eternal law, of the laws of God–those laws which were before Abraham and which will be until the end of the world. You will begin to understand yourself and your place in God's scheme.

Does anyone here believe that he came to this earth just to go to school and get married and raise a family and die? You see what I mean? That leaves the whole idea of God out of it, doesn't it? I mean, no matter how happy and how harmonious your human experience can be–and many people have wonderful ones–could that really be God's plan for his creation? Isn't that really too insignificant to credit to Deity? This class can't end Friday night if you will meditate on your individual place in God's scheme, in God's plan.

What is God's plan for the spiritual universe? What is God's plan for that thing we call earth? The only answer can come from within your own being because it concerns your place in that scheme. It concerns your place in life. None of us out here in the outer world will ever find our spiritual place unless we learn it from within, unless we receive from within the impulse that gradually lead us to that place.

Let us get on for a minute to this subject of spiritual healing. Spiritual healing is accomplished only when there is no resistance in the healer's thought to the condition or the person. "Agree with thine adversary whilst thou art on the way with him."[3] In much healing work where there is a denial and an affirmation, there is set up immediately a resistance to the error. Remember that the error isn't a thing and it isn't a condition and it isn't a person, so in setting up that resistance, you are almost creating the thing you are resisting.

In spiritual healing, you have to recognize that error does not exist as a reality, no matter what form it appears in—sin, disease, lack or limitation. When the problem is presented to you, do not resist it, do not deny it or affirm it. Just take the attitude of non-resistance, divine indifference—not putting out a mental wall against it, not trying to overcome it, not trying to deny it—just having an attitude of freedom from fear, an attitude of realizing that you don't have to resist a mirage, an attitude that you are not going to separate the railroad tracks or lift the sky off the mountain. Yet don't wait for that moment to take that attitude, for that will be affirmation and denial and to that degree will be resistance.

Please try to remember that at this moment I am giving you just about the top level of spiritual healing that we can realize right now. It is as if Jesus were facing a man with a withered arm and saying, "Stretch forth your hand!"[4] What would make it possible for him to say that to a man with a withered arm? Or to the cripple, "Rise! Pick up thy bed and walk!"[5] It would only be because he recognized not just in that minute, but his whole life was a constant recognition, that there wasn't anything to hinder you. He knew there wasn't any presence or power in the arm or the leg or in the back that had anything to do with rising and picking up your bed and walking.

Try to visualize now what I mean when I say, "Give me some help." Instead of reacting with, "What do I think about this? What do I know? It isn't true, it isn't

real," just smile, knowing that you are being presented
with a mirage and that all you have to do is recognize
that it is a mirage. I am trying, in the three nights that we
have left, to present every phase of this activity to you,
not merely to show you as we did last night what treatment is, what prayer is, but also to give you the very
highest idea of which I am capable at the moment, of
that which constitutes spiritual healing.

You see, this Christ-consciousness does not resist
error. Why? Because it doesn't recognize error as a
power. You remember Jesus to Pilate, "Thou couldest
have no power over me unless it came from the
Father."[6] Even in walking on the water Jesus did not
recognize the power of his body to sink.

Spiritual consciousness is one which does not accept
any belief in thought of any error existing as a presence
or as a power. It looks at any presence or form or phase
of error as if it were just looking at a moving picture, say,
of a man being shot, knowing right well that as soon as
the picture is over, the man is going to pick himself up
and dust himself off and get ready to play another part.
That is somewhat the mental attitude you have when
you are looking at a horror picture but sitting back and
knowing all the time it is just a movie and therefore you
don't allow yourself to have any feelings of sympathy
with the underdog, or you don't go mellow on the hero.
You are just sitting there in the realization that you are
watching the unfolding of fiction, of a myth.

In maintaining that same attitude toward what we see
of human experience, that same attitude in which we do
not criticize or judge or condemn the underdog or the
sinning or sick person, and in which we do not give
praise to those we think are doing good, we will have

begun to see real spiritual healing. In recognizing all good as coming from God and all evil as the mirage, we have Christ healing–the same type of healing done by Jesus and the disciples without taking thought, without the use of a power to overcome any evil. When that state of consciousness is with us, we are then getting to that place where every call for help rouses in us nothing more and nothing less than, "What can I do about a mirage?"

~ 17 ~

OPENING CONSCIOUSNESS TO TRUTH

TONIGHT WE ARE GOING TO START with a short period of meditation, but it will be a different meditation than we have had before, in that instead of taking the word into consciousness and pondering it, this time we just will open consciousness and listen. We will just open consciousness for that inflow. We can visualize it this way. Using the illustration of Niagara Falls and Lake Erie, we will suppose here that I am Niagara Falls and in and of myself I am continuously using up myself so that ultimately there would be nothing left, especially in three or four years or ten or twenty. Instead of that, let us know that behind me, as Niagara Falls, there is Lake Erie. As a matter of fact, actually there is no Niagara Falls–Niagara Falls is only a name given to Lake Erie at one corner where it goes over the Falls.

Now, so with us. We call ourselves man, but actually we aren't. We are God, but that which is visible of us here is God where God becomes visible, where God comes to a focus, you may say, in an individual yet infinite manner. In other words, it is like realizing that Niagara Falls and Lake Erie are not two but one, and all that Lake Erie is, of course, Niagara is; all that Lake Erie has, Niagara has. But Lake Erie is continuously pouring itself forth as Niagara.

So with us. God is forever pouring itself forth as individual you and me. There is really no place where God ends and man begins. I and the Father are one, and that is the meaning of this. There is no place where you can separate us and say here is God and here is man, any more than you can say that up to there is Lake Erie and from here on is Niagara Falls. There is no such place in the whole watershed.

Now, since it is true that all of the Godhead is pouring itself forth as individual you and me, the only reason for any lack in our experience, whether it is lack of health or lack of wealth or a lack of opportunity or a lack of any form, is the fact that we have come to believe that this is all there is of us, that this is our being, instead of our merely being that place through which all of God is pouring forth. Now, to correct that mistake, to overcome that belief of separation, there is only one thing necessary: that our consciousness be open at all times for the inflow—Lake Erie—God—to flow out as me or as you.

This work is a conscious work. It is not one in which you can just sit around and say, "Well, let God do it." There comes a time when you do say, "I'm just letting God do it," and the statement is all right. But at this particular stage, if we were to say, "Oh, let God do it," we would be thinking of something separate and apart from our own being as if it were going to do something for us, whereas the attitude is a very scientific one, "Let God do it!" That attitude at this moment could be so badly mistaken that we would lose our whole path through blind faith.

Now then, let us open our consciousness and take the attitude of Samuel: "Speak, Father; thy servant heareth..."[1] or Mrs. Eddy's hymn: "I Will Listen For

Thy Voice . . ." or the Bible: " . . . listening to the still small voice . . ."² or "Be still and know that the I is God . . ."³ and that the I is pouring itself forth as the individual me.

The object, then, of this meditation will be (remember our basic statement: "Seek ye first the kingdom of God and his rightness and all things will be added . . ."⁴) not to demonstrate a single thing, a single person, or a single condition. We are just going to open consciousness in the realization that Lake Erie is flowing right across that place called Niagara Falls that is still Lake Erie appearing as Niagara Falls–and actually that God is pouring itself forth as Joel Goldsmith and there is no place that God ends and the man begins. There is no place where God ends and you begin; it is all one continuous flow.

After we have done that, we are going to make this a continuous thing. There is going to be no two-a-day about this! From this point on, after we meditate tonight, we are going to open our consciousness to the truth that "I and the Father are one."⁵ Especially after we get into bed and especially before we get out of bed in the morning, and then as many hours through the day as we can, we are going to remember, "I and the Father are one," and that this Lake Erie is pouring itself forth as me.

Even if we do not sit down to meditate, we shall, for a second or a minute, open our consciousness to the realization of this relationship between God–the infinite invisible–and ourselves, the visible manifestation of that infinite invisible.

"Thou wilt keep him in perfect peace whose mind is stayed on thee . . ."⁶ and we are going to keep our consciousness stayed on God from now on through the rest of time–not in any foolish, stupid way, but in just this way of every hour at least–opening our ears, or just

looking up toward the skies, which will be our recognition of the infinitude of God pouring forth as individual
me.

A month from now you will look in the mirror and
you won't know yourself! As you sit in meditation you
will notice a change taking place within your system. For
one thing, as your breathing slows down (and it will) and
your thoughts race less and less and finally cease, you
will probably find that your diaphragm will go in and
your chest come out much like an athlete's figure. It just
seems to draw itself in at the waist and the chest comes
up and gives you that pose. Probably that is the normal
position of the body. Anyway, it does happen, and it
brings a beautiful sense of peace with it. Your ideal
meditation comes in at that point because from there on
you do not think a single thought. The rhythm of the
universe is taking possession of you; you may not move,
but you feel that you are in tune, you feel there's a
rhythm, you feel there is a harmony of being and of
mental peace. It is more than a mental peace; it is a
spiritual peace which settles upon you and you could
really sit there for many, many minutes in that attitude.

Do not let that become the attitude of falling asleep.
Do not let it become an attitude of mental laziness,
because this that I am describing is the opposite of that;
what I am describing is a spirit of alertness in which you
do no thinking. You just seem to rest back in peace and
harmony but become receptive to impartation from
within. You will find many passages in the Bible describing that beautiful peace that comes when we feel held by
the everlasting arms, when the soul is at rest, when the
soul senses are at rest. Remember, it is not to be mental
stagnation, it is not to be a falling asleep. It is a wonderful

alertness, yet containing the feel of the "peace that passeth understanding." We feel the joy of being without any external reason for that joy; it is an inner attunement.

Ultimately, you will do every bit of your healing work in that way. Ultimately, you will come to that place where you will not take a single thought when you sit down to help anyone or even to help yourself. You may remind yourself, of course, that there is no place where Lake Erie ends and Niagara Falls begins, no place where God ends and you begin. "All of the Godhead is pouring forth as me; all that the Father hath is mine; all of the wisdom, all of the knowledge, all that I need to know, is omnipresent as my very own consciousness. With a few little reminders like that, and, "Speak, Father, for thy servant heareth" and "Here am I, waiting for the still small voice . . ." until gradually that sense of peace comes and you just stay there in that peace until the click comes, and then you are through. You will know that the patient has either had a healing or has felt a great sense of relief or freedom or that the situation has been met in some way. If you are called on to do it over again and over again, it is still the same thing–finding the center of your being, finding your oneness with the eternal, feeling the complete rhythm of this universe–and yourself in tune with it.

Now, there is a spiritual law underlying that; there is a spiritual law underlying this sense of peace or meditation in which no thought takes place, no argument, no treatment–just the conscious awareness of God's presence. It is another illustration of how the Bible is full of tremendous laws that we just use as quotations.

"Resist not evil!"[7] Have you ever heard about that one? Oh, yes! There is one of the most powerful laws in

the entire Bible! Resist not evil! Why? It is not real and
if you resist it, you make it real. What a battle you have
then! Resist not evil! In the face of any erroneous
picture, in the face of any discord, instead of denying it,
instead of saying it isn't happening (how foolish, for it is
happening out in that picture) let's not argue, let's not
fight it, let's not resist it at all, but just sit back and say, "I
wonder how real you could be?" Resist not evil is the
acme of spiritual healing. It enables you to face any
situation in the world and almost say, "So what?"

You see, since our premise is that all action is mind
action and God is the only mind, everything that is
appearing to you is the activity of God. So what we are
doing now is not overcoming error, but rightly interpreting that picture before us. Inasmuch as it is foolish for us
to sit and look at a sin or disease and say, "You are
God's perfect image," I really think that is stretching it
a little too far. Still it is quite in order to say, "How about
interpreting this for me and letting me see it as it is?" It
is perfectly all right to say that to God—no resistance
there, you see; no acknowledgment that it is an error to
be overcome. No acknowledgment that there is a sinner
to be reformed; no acknowledgment that there is a lack
or limitation that must be met; just that here is somebody talking in Sanskrit and the only interpreter is God,
so you have to let God interpret this hodge-podge of
black print before you! You see, in spiritual healing
there is no mental action, there is no conscious thought-
taking, there is no conscious affirming or denying. There
is more of the sense that inasmuch as the reality of this
is of and in God, I am going to let God interpret it to
me.

You can take that same attitude when you are reading
a book or reading the Bible or listening to a lecture or to

a teacher. You can sit back there too, and say, "I am not so much interested in what you are saying as in how God is going to interpret it to me." Then you can sit back quietly not using the thing up in the head called brain. You let your state of receptivity take in what is being said or read, then you let the infinite within you translate it for you.

How many here have actually done, say, one month of this kind of work on the quotation, "Resist not evil"? You must know it is the law of God or it wouldn't be in that Book the way it is. We just say, "I don't understand that." We somehow get the idea that if we are not to resist evil, we will succumb to temptation and before we know it we will be stealing or committing adultery. This is not so. Let us resist not evil *because* evil isn't any thing or person. It is a misinterpretation of some activity of God since God is, literally, all. Since there is no action apart from mind action, since there is no activity apart from eternal life, even in looking at what the world calls death, we are actually witnessing eternal life in action.

That is the only way Jesus could raise anyone from the dead. That is the only way a practitioner can raise the dying back to life—not by saying, "You are dying, but I am going to raise you back to life," but by recognizing that there is nothing going on here but the activity of mind; that he must just sit in peace and quiet until God, the inner interpreter of his being, interprets it for him.

You see, we don't do the interpreting. There is some of that metaphysical work that I sometimes get a little bit too angry about, where we are supposed to turn around and say, "It isn't true or it isn't real or all this is nonsense!" What are we saying it for if it isn't? We believe it is, or we wouldn't be saying it isn't.

I never knew of a millionaire who went around saying, "I'm rich and I know it." That is usually done by the fellow who isn't rich and who is trying to hypnotize himself into the belief that he is. You don't find many healthy people going around saying, "I am well; I am God's perfect child!" And you don't find nicely employed people saying, "God is my employer!" No! They have the actual consciousness of it! They don't have to go around deluding themselves with a lot of statements that they hope to make come true.

Rather, when you are faced with what appears to your sense to be evil, be honest about it. Be sure that you do not make empty denials and statements that you wish were true. You will find that you have a lot more respect for your own metaphysics when you are making statements that you yourself believe and when you do not go around making a lot of statements which in the back of your mind you do not believe but wish were true.

All of these statements have been stepping-stones, but for a lot of people they have been stepping-stones to the grave, or to an institution or to an accident. For some people who were wise enough to see that statements were just temporary measures out of which they had to develop, they were really stepping-stones into something better. You see, in this field like in everything else, we are up against the fact that the average person isn't an independent thinker. He is more apt to be a blotting paper, willing just to absorb what somebody says or somebody writes. For that reason you will hear students make all the ridiculous statements found in print–and how many of those there are!

From here let us say, "From now on I am going at least to be honest! I am not going around saying I am rich if I am hungry, or well if I am sick. From now on I will make the open admission that I feel terrible and I am hungry, but I know right well there is a right interpretation to this thing. There is a right answer and I am going to sit down and meditate and let God get me back on the beam." It is all right if you catch this idea that because the activity of mind is all there is, that even that which is appearing to be a discord is some part of God's allness; it is perfectly all right to assure yourself or reassure yourself with, "Wait! I don't have to believe this picture, since I do know that in the nature of reality all is good. So now let me sit back and realize it. Let me receive the divine impartation that will dispel the illusion."

Let me tell you one great truth: that no amount of this kind of work up here in the head is going to heal your disease or your lack. You might as well make up your mind to that right here and now, that mental power is not Christ-power. Christ-power is gentleness and peace and all-knowing and confidence and understanding. It has nothing to do with battling.

I love the passage in that little book *Grace* that we read here Saturday, and which said something to the effect that the nature of the Christ knows no battle. There, too, the Bible shows us that, "Stand you still and see the salvation of the Lord[8] . . . The battle is not yours, but God's."[9] So, you see, there is no need for all this mental battling. We who have come to this place are here because we are ready to give up our mental processes. That is what has drawn us here together. We are in one place and of one mind and nobody pulled us in. We came here through some divine urge within our own being and we wouldn't be here if we weren't ready, I can assure you of that.

Let us—even while we are reviewing these notes, even
while we are finding wonderful statements to buoy us up
at times—let us really know that these are just temporary
stopgaps and that they are just reminders to sit back and
let God, let the infinite intelligence of your being, interpret this thing to you. I said before that the earth is really
heaven, only seen through finite sense, seen through a
"glass darkly." Well, inasmuch as you will never see it
any other way than that with your eyes, why not acknowledge it and sit back with your eyes closed and let your
spiritual sense reveal the harmony of being to you.

Here again I come to a very important point. It isn't
our human saying that God is all that brings out a
demonstration for us. There must be the development of
the spiritual sense, what I call soul sense, so that you
perceive that which is not visible or tangible to the five
senses. You perceive it through your inner, soul sense.
Oh, in a measure, you catch a glimpse of that when you
have the faculty of looking at a person and saying,
"That's an honest person," or "I would not trust this
person!" How do you know? You don't know that with
your brain. Some little inner thing shows you all of that.
The same thing happens when you really are watchful in
your reading. You should have no difficulty in recognizing a statement that comes right out of the consciousness
of truth and one that is someone's human opinion (or
somebody's quotation of somebody else without having
had any consciousness of it). Something within you
should respond and say, "That is true," or "I would not
want to bother with this kind of statement." Something
within you does it—and that something is the soul sense.

Remember, we said that hearing, seeing, tasting,
touching and smelling are our concepts of the spiritual

activity of consciousness; therefore, the five physical senses represent our misconception of the real soul faculty. Now, we all have soul faculty. There would not be one of us spending human time on divine spiritual subjects if this were not so, for it would be a waste of time to material sense. Only to us it is not a waste of time, it is an investment! But to the material sense, all of this would be a waste of time. We wouldn't be here but for the fact that we have some measure of spiritual consciousness, we have some measure of spiritual sense. It is that measure, it is that spiritual sense, that makes you enjoy this and makes me enjoy it. It is that spirit—it is not our human intellect. Our intellect would rebel at this; I know too many people with the fine human intellects and I know how they would rebel, and you do, too. No, you must have some measure of developed spiritual sense to be able to sit and listen or read for very long on these metaphysical subjects. What I mean to be saying is that we must increase the measure of our soul sense, of our spiritual sense, and we must do that by looking at any appearance and letting God translate it into its spiritual significance.

When, as sometimes happens, we have fore-vision—foresight—or catch a glimpse of some scene or event which has not happened yet but which usually happens the next day or the next week or the next month—inasmuch as we are recognizing God as the only mind, we know well that what is coming to us is the misinterpretation of the activity of the divine mind. We must understand it can be so and immediately declare that this is only the finite, human sense of some spiritual activity. Then, sit for a few moments and let the divine mind reinterpret that vision.

There was a time when I did not know how to do this
(I was just a youngster) and I had some very unpleasant
experiences. My father was a European traveler and
spent much of his time over there. I went to my mother
one day and said, "Mom, something is wrong in Europe;
something is wrong with Pop!" There wasn't anything
we could do about it because all we knew was that he
had just landed in England. But the next day we had a
cable from him that he was on his way between two
stations in London to catch the Nottingham express and
for the first time in 100 trips he missed his train. That
was when the Nottingham express was wrecked and
everyone aboard was killed–101 people! It just happened that I had nothing to do with the fact that he
missed the train; my vision did not help because I did
not know how to handle it. A short time after that I said
to my mother, "There is a railroad wreck in Connecti-
cut." This was verified in the paper that night. I still
didn't know how to handle it.

Later on I always caught a certain signal when
someone was about to pass on–someone I knew, someone in the family, a close friend. I never knew or understood anything about it, but always the passing came
after that signal. It was only after I learned in Science
how to reverse these things that I learned how, once the
signal came, to reverse it and prevent its happening.
This happened once in the Midwest when a woman
came up to me in a department store and asked the
buyer to whom I was talking to introduce her. She told
me that one of my family close to me would die that
week and it would be either from heart disease or an
automobile accident–she wasn't quite sure which. At
that time I was a student of Science and I knew how to

avert this. I got busy right there and then in the realization that God was the only presence and the only power and that the only activity that could take place was the activity of mind, and all this was merely like a sin or a disease; it was just the negative appearance and just the reverse of that which was actually happening. That member of my family was in an automobile a few days later, going around a curve, went up on two wheels and then came back on four again. That was the end of that; there was no death that time. Soon after that I was in the practice and again, every time some patient was in danger, I got that signal. From then on I knew how to avert the danger or the death. I knew that all of these pictures—we call them premonitions—were misinterpretations of divine activity.

You must turn to your divine mind, your infinite intelligence, and realize that no picture appears before you except that picture which is painted by the hand of the divine and is good. If there is any other picture appearing, it is merely the misinterpretation of that divine activity. Keep up your work until you get the feeling that you do with a healing. Even with a good picture, do the same. You don't want anything but divinity itself! Otherwise, if you were a practitioner, all you would want would be that your patient become well, or you might get him well today and find that something else occurs tomorrow.

No, we don't want physical health. I don't mean that we *un*-want it. I mean that is not the object of our work. Just because a patient says, "I have no fever" and "My body seems all right," that isn't our work. Our work even then is to realize that even the appearance of physical health is only a misinterpretation of the divine health which is life eternal. That goes back to "New

Horizon" in the book *The Infinite Way*. Every human picture is mesmeric suggestion, every human picture is a finite presentation of the infinite—even the good ones! Even the good ones! Ask some of your millionaires whether they think it so good to be a millionaire. Ask some of the healthy people whether they are happy or contented. No, every human picture!

We are here because we have risen to that point where we are not satisfied to make sick people well people just through some kind of process; that is not the end and object of our work. The end and object of our work is to reverse the whole human picture so that we can see you as you divinely are—that means eternal and immortal. Any picture that is presented to the sight, good or bad, should have the immediate recognition that God is the author and the creator; it is infinitely good and what is appearing finitely is but the false interpretation of that infinite, beautiful picture which we can't see with our physical eyes but which internally we can feel with our spiritual sense.

This is a very important thing. I don't want to leave here tomorrow night with any misgiving about that. Here is one point where this particular presentation goes far beyond ordinary metaphysical practice. We are not concerned merely with making unemployed people employed or demonstrating money for them or demonstrating a perfect heart for them. Our work goes far beyond that; it goes into the realm of bringing to light the spiritual selfhood of the individual—and this is unchanging, undying. Only by this realization do we achieve this. Don't believe what your eyes see, that is what I am trying to tell you—even if it is a good picture. It is always only a finite interpretation of the infinitely real which is there waiting to be spiritually discerned, waiting to be realized with your spiritual senses–with the sense of feeling.

* * * * * *

Question: *What did you mean in the San Francisco lecture series by saying: "I am the light of the world and, you see, I am the light of the world for the benefit of those who at the moment may seem to be enjoying some phase of darkness. When they are no longer enjoying it, they will come out from under."*

Answer: The question there probably had something to do with enjoying some phase of darkness. Of course, that was half cynical and half true. In this sense is it true: even when we are enjoying good health and even when we are enjoying good supply, we are just enjoying darkness *if* it is physical health and physical wealth that we are enjoying.

This truth has come to be the light even to that. This truth that we are presenting isn't merely to make sick people well or poor people rich, but to awaken even healthy and wealthy people to a dependence on spiritual power, on spiritual security, on spiritual freedom. That is the difference we gave when we spoke to another audience the other day. That is the difference between Moses who gave the Jews a bigger place to live, more food, greater religious freedom, and a lot of other human freedoms, but never gave them the spiritual freedom that would have made them eternally free. And Jesus: Jesus came along to do that and the Hebrews could not accept him and they missed the boat. All are Hebrews in the sense that they are clinging to economic security and to political security and who feel more safe with a Republican in the White House than with a Communist there—these with dependence on political person and ideology, but who have not yet found this spiritual security which would keep them safe regardless of where they were or who was governing.

Our particular approach presents this main difference from any other metaphysical teaching and that is why it is not on the level of the human. It is trying to awaken even healthy humans and wealthy humans from their dependence on physical security, on physical health and physical happiness.

To be a Christian means more than merely membership in a Christian organization or citizenship in a Christian country. It means living the Christ principle. To live the Christ principle means literally to pray for our enemies, to pray for those who persecute us or despitefully use us; it means a sincere effort to forgive our debtors even unto seventy times seven; to return love for hate. The Christ life compels us to put up the sword and therefore to use no human force even in our defense.

Of course you understand we are not to dictate our will to our neighbor and if our nation calls upon us for warfare or for the means of conducting war, we are to render unto Caesar that which is Caesar's. We can fulfill every demand made upon us and yet do it with no malice or hate or fear and with no conviction that force is a real power. The Christian life is an individual one and is never forced upon another. All are Christians who accept the law and reality of spiritual power, whether they belong to other churches or none. Christians have no occasion to rely on human means and methods since they have the inner presence to guide, direct, govern, heal, maintain and protect. They have "meat ye know not of "[10]—an inner reliance.

Most Christians are more Hebraic than Christian. They believe in the Judaic teachings. Most Christians do. Most Christians have more knowledge of and faith in what is in the Old Testament than in what is in the New. When you tell a Christian that you dare not throw an ill-word to your neighbor, no matter what his offense to you, they take that as something transcendental rather than as an actual teaching of Jesus Christ. When you talk to Christians about praying for their enemies, they don't seem to know that those passages are in the Bible or that we are consciously to act upon those laws. No, they don't do it; Christians are not always Christian. They read that story of the good Samaritan and yet they will withhold help from somebody for a personal reason. Maybe he is German, maybe he is Japanese or he is Catholic or a man of another color—or a woman. They consider those good reasons for withholding help. But whatever it is, they are not fulfilling the teaching of the Christ, the teaching of the Master. His teachings unveil and reveal to us spiritual being, spiritual identity, spiritual existence. Do you see what I mean?

I really do not believe that metaphysicians read the Bible enough. Or, when they do read it, they do not take such passages and say, "What kind of law is being revealed? Is this just a story in the book? What is its meaning for me here?" I am so grateful for the unfoldment of the *Spiritual Interpretation of Scripture*. Now when I read a piece of Scripture—whether in our Bible or in any of the older Bibles—I say to myself, "What does it mean?" That one, "Resist not evil." Just think of that one!

All over the land we are told how to protect ourselves from evil—what to do about it when we meet up with it—while all the time it is our own imagination backfiring.

Resist not evil! When someone calls for help don't put up a mental barrier and deny evil. Your denial is power. You know back in your consciousness that it can't be true or real and that in itself is a denial without voicing it.

Instead of taking the time to deny it, sit back and with your spiritual sense reinterpret it; let God reinterpret whatever the picture is before you. Then you can say, "It really isn't real and I've seen it demonstrated . . . I have seen the unreality demonstrated and made manifest. Since I am infinite consciousness and include within my own being the entire universe, I—through my consciousness of this truth—become the law unto that universe. If I behold evil and start to fight it and battle with it, I make it a reality and I give it a power that may make it impossible for me ever to overcome it. On the other hand, if I accept in my consciousness that evil is unreal and therefore does not have to be resisted or battled, I can afford to spend my time in silent meditation, in peaceful enjoyment of the spiritual laws of life. I become a law unto my universe by my conscious attitude toward the universe.

If I resist those who wrong me, I set that wrong up as an antagonism and even if that individual did not harm me, some other one would come along and do it. This would occur merely because I had set up that antagonism as something of a real nature that had to be battled or overcome. If, however, I can see all injustice, all lack of integrity, all inharmony, all discord, all lack of cooperative action, as merely the finite interpretation of that which is real, then—instead of battling it—I merely sit back quietly, resist not evil, and become the law over that situation and watch it automatically dissolve. That same person who has done me seeming wrong or injustice will dissolve all the feelings he might have had.

If you stand on your human rights or even on your legal rights, you'll find yourself in a battle. Our word is not to battle. Stand still and see the salvation of the truth that God is all that is ever appearing in circumstance or condition. But as we see it, even when it is good, it represents our finite sense of it.

Remember the import of tonight's lesson—it is covered, too, in "New Horizon" of *The Infinite Way*. It is covered now in another way, another angle, another sense—so that you can see that we are not to be satisfied even with good human pictures, we are immediately to translate them. We are not to be satisfied by human health, physical health. We are not to be satisfied with physical wealth. Don't be satisfied, either, with the mere fact that you have a loyal wife, a loyal husband, a loyal friend. Sometimes when your dependence is in the human you find humans turn on you. They do that very often. But, if we are always reversing that picture and saying, "I know that every bit of good here is the infinite good of God individualizing itself in my experience, that all of this good coming to me is God's good," then we have nothing to fear. We don't have to rest there and hope that this good human is going to keep on being good or friendly or honest. Do you follow that?

The whole essence tonight is: Do not let us either be good humans or be satisfied with good humanness! Let us not be engaged in a ministry of making sick people well or poor people rich when actually our work is that of spiritual unfoldment; don't let us get into that ministry. Why? I'll tell you why. You'll learn it, too, as you keep on contemplating that letter you received tonight; you'll begin to understand that we, here, have in some way been chosen.

~ 18 ~

MYSTICISM

THE TRUE MEANING OF MYSTICISM is any teaching, any philosophy, or any religion that adheres to oneness with God. It is conscious oneness with God, the ability to receive impartations or guidance direct from God. It is the ability to commune with God, to be consciously at one with God, the ability to receive good from God individually and directly. We may sum it all up, then, in saying that mysticism is any teaching that brings out oneness with God, and this teaching of ours stresses, above all things else, oneness with God—conscious oneness with God.

I want to start right off with a great secret. You will find this in my writings, but you will also find that it has not been taken too seriously by those who have read it. It has probably not, except in a few cases, been recognized as one of the supreme wisdoms of the world. This has occurred, firstly, because it is not stated in mystical language but in plain English and secondly, because people are not in the habit of analyzing statements.

I am now going to give you the highest mystical statement that I know—one that will absolutely provide you with a passkey to heaven, to harmony of mind and body and business, health, wealth and all other things.

That statement is: *Oneness with God constitutes oneness with all spiritual being and things.* Oneness with God constitutes oneness with all spiritual being and things. You might realize, "My oneness with God constitutes my oneness with all spiritual being and things," and that is a passport right into wealth and health. Why? We go back to the illustration of the telephone. You can't get anywhere in the world on the telephone without going to the central office, but once you contact the central office, you can contact any place on the face of the globe that has a telephone.

Now, this truth is a higher truth than any telephone system. If you contact God, if once you make your conscious realization with God, then automatically and instantaneously you are at one with the entire universe of spiritual idea. Everything that we see, hear, touch or smell is really just a finite concept of divine idea. For instance, an automobile—an automobile isn't so much! Just one little piece of transportation. If you have one, it will wear out or run down or become obsolete; it will require another investment to replace it. But, behind the *idea* of automobile or behind the object, automobile, there is the divine idea of transportation. Transportation is really a spiritual activity; it is an activity of mind imparting itself as idea to individual being.

Of course, if you once contact God, or spirit, you have contacted the law, the spiritual law of transportation. Therefore, if your need for an automobile is a real one, you will be surprised how quickly you will obtain one—or an airplane or seat in an airplane or a steamship ticket or a passport—or anything that has to do with transportation. These would immediately be available to you because of your oneness with the source, the infinite source of all good.

Now, we should not attempt to demonstrate an automobile. The point is this: Let us say that I am in San Francisco and my home is in Los Angeles. In a human sense I must bridge that four hundred odd miles and so I have need of transportation—or that is the way the problem would appear to me. Suppose I have no immediate solution to the problem. I sit down and realize my oneness with God and realize it in as many different ways as I can. I may think of the wave as one with the ocean, of the sunbeam as one with the sun. I may think of the selfhood that is one with God and the motherhood and fatherhood that is one with God.

In any way that I can I relate myself to God until finally I come into the realization that "All that the Father hath is mine because we are one." I realize that there is no separation between God and man—God and man are one, "I and the Father are one; all that the Father hath is right here where I am!" If I achieve that realization, if I obtain that inner sense of peace that we call the click, the realization, very quickly I will find that my transportation to Los Angeles appears. It may be an invitation to ride with someone; it may be a railroad ticket; it may be someone down there sending for me. Whatever appears could appear in any way. However, I would not at any time have to think about transportation. I would have to think about my oneness with God and about the immediate availability of God in every form. In the same way, let us take a person seeking truth. Everyone who has turned his thought in this path is seeking truth. What such persons want is the highest unfoldment there is for their state of consciousness. They want that unfoldment which will meet their particular needs.

There is a library here with thousands of books in it. You might read every one of those books out there but one and not find your need met. All that reading might be wasted, too, because it would be just as easy to go to the center of your being and there realize that God and truth are synonymous and, since you are one with God, you are one with truth—that all the truth in the universe is available to you. Not available tomorrow—but now! Available right here, right where you are. There is no time, place or space from which you can be separated from truth, from all the truth in the universe, because you can't be separated from God.

As you pondered so day in and day out, you would be led to just the one book that really would open the floodgates to you. From there on, you would be led to book after book, teacher after teacher, but only to those who were in accord with your own consciousness, those that would meet your particular need. Do you see what I mean? There is no need to read every book in the world to find the truth you need. You can be led to just those authors, just those teachers, just those scriptures that follow your particular line of truth.

The same thing can happen when we need a home (or want a home or are ready for a home) or want to move somewhere else. Again, we are not using this truth to demonstrate a house or a place to live; but if this truth did not bring us fulfillment of harmony, it would not be the truth of being because Christ said, "I am come that ye may have life and have it more abundantly; I am come that ye might be fulfilled,"[1] and of course, a home and companionship and those things are part of our fulfillment.

Having arrived at a place where we know that, and we know that our desires run in that direction, let us now forget the home and the house and all the rest. Let us turn within and again realize God. Realize that the only home there is, is in our own consciousness, that we live and move and have our being in God—in true consciousness. True consciousness is omnipresent as our own being. As we realize the true nature of spiritual home with all the qualities of home, such as protection, love, joy, beauty, cooperativeness, safety, security, the first thing we know, our home appears; for our conscious oneness with God is what brings it into manifestation, not our going outside to demonstrate things.

Remember always that the basis of our work is, "Seek ye first the kingdom of God."[2] One of those ways of seeking first the kingdom of God is this realization, because when we have demonstrated our conscious oneness with God, all the things are added unto us. Therefore, oneness with God constitutes oneness with every spiritual being. There may be the need for some person to bring about the happy adjustment of our affairs—it maybe the right real estate agent or the right banker or else the right metaphysical teacher; it may be a need for the right kind of investment counselor or any type person—anywhere. We would contact the right one not by desiring the right one, but by consciously realizing our oneness with God.

A wonderful thing happened to me this morning. I wish you had all been with me then. This lesson poured itself into my consciousness at that time. It just poured itself into me and poured in and poured in. I kept saying, "Why aren't they here right now?" I wish sometimes I were like the Hindu swamis in India who have their students come and live with them for three years. Then at three o'clock in the morning, if they feel like talking, they send word out to get them all up. When they meet, the Swami talks and talks, perhaps until five o'clock, and then they go back to bed. If the Swami feels that at seven o'clock he is ready to talk again, out come the students at seven o'clock. You never know at what hour of day or night you are going to be summoned into the Holy Presence to hear the divine pearls of wisdom that flow from God.

You would have heard some this morning, for I just seemed afire with all this—but this is what came to me in the midst of it: "Inasmuch as I am consciously one with God, I must be consciously one with the individual consciousness of everyone here. Certainly they, too, must be receiving the same message I am receiving." I would not have been at all surprised if some of you had said tonight, "Why, I know a lot! I heard it this morning sometime." That is the idea—someone seemed to be telling it to me. Ultimately, you see, those of us who follow the mystical path are going to learn that it isn't really necessary to talk as much as we do. We will all receive the messages and the impartations necessary for us with much less conversation, and that brings us to one of the questions of the morning.

In our human experience we are continuously making human contacts upon whom we depend a great deal to bring us this or that. We are depending a great deal on word of mouth reputation and on repetition, and so forth and so on, in this mystical approach that is about as unnecessary as buying a meal right after you come from a banquet. Because in the mystical approach where you realize that God the infinite intelligence of the universe has really created in you an idea to sell—whether it is metaphysical teaching, metaphysical healing, ice-boxes or property, whatever it is—then you realize that you yourself are not the creator of it even if you invented a machine to carry through with the idea. That does not make any difference; it was really the activity and operation of divine mind, universal intelligence, that did it all.

It took place as the activity of mind, but it also took place in that universal mind. Is that universal mind anything but your mind and mine? Therefore, it automatically took place in the mind of every one of us at the same time. It is needless to advertise it. The very moment that the divine mind implanted an idea in what I call individual being—let's say, an idea of this unfolding truth—we know that it is automatically implanted in your consciousness. That's why you're here to get it. It is only that you haven't been trained to bring it forth out of your consciousness and so you are coming to have it unveiled for you.

You must at least know that I am not telling you anything that is not already a part of your consciousness. If I were, you could not understand it. I might just as well sit up here and talk in Sanskrit—you wouldn't get it. That is only because Sanskrit is not yet needed as a conscious activity of your experience. But, if you were at that level of consciousness where Sanskrit was a necessity, why, you would be led right to that person who could teach it to you—there is no question about that.

Now, always remember this: Nobody can ever give you anything that isn't already a part of your consciousness. Therefore, nobody is up here giving you anything. He is unveiling it for you—it is within your own consciousness. That is why (and here is where we can have a nice prayer of thanks!), it would not have mattered whether or not I came to San Francisco. This truth that you already felt would have come forth in you this very week. It would not have made any difference whether I had come or not. Somebody else would have given it to you, or you would have found the book that would have had it, or, if there was no other way, God would have hit you over the head and said, "Here! Wake up, I'm talking to you!" You would have heard it in your sleep or as you were walking down the street. Never believe that this truth has anything to do with a person's coming to San Francisco to give it to you or that it is lucky he came here or that you are glad he came here. You can be glad, but not necessarily for that; you would have gotten it anyhow.

If that weren't true, then Jesus was all wrong when he said, "If I go not away, the Comforter will not come to you."[3] In other words, if this message were dependent upon a person—"Oh my, where is God? Where is God in all that picture?" Just think! Here I am in San Francisco, but there are many thousands of cities all over the United States where I am not. Is God cheating those people, do you think? Don't you delude yourself. Every person in this world who is ready for this message is receiving it this minute!

That is the benefit of mysticism. You see, your conscious oneness with God makes everything in this world available the moment that you want it. Nobody can keep it away from you, either—nobody! And if you are not following the path of God, I don't mind telling you, you are going to fail in the end, anyhow. Perhaps it is just as well if you fail in the beginning and save a lot of heartaches. No! Conscious union with God is mysticism. Conscious oneness with God constitutes your oneness with all spiritual being, with every spiritual idea.

Take money. Money is just a human concept—but it is a human concept of a divine idea; it represents love, gratitude, sharing, cooperativeness. So, as a spiritual idea, you know it can't come to you; it must be an embodied idea and activity of your consciousness. One of the reasons why we are short of money when we are short of it, is that we are looking for it to come to us when it is hidden in our own consciousness all the time. That is the way it is. We are often trying to demonstrate something that is already part of our own consciousness all the time; it is already within us and we are looking for it in a person, in a place, in a thing.

We all know that there are many, many stories of the search for the Holy Grail, for that gold cup that Jesus is supposed to have drunk from at the Crucifixion. In every story of this search, the man who is searching finally comes home, denuded of money, broken in health. He comes home and drops wearily and despondently at his own door—and then he finds it! In every instance the story describes a person who gives his whole life and fortune to the search in the outer world and each time he finds it on his return home; he finds it in his garden, perhaps, hanging to a branch of a tree. He reaches forth his hand at his own table and it appears. This is all symbolic and means that the Holy Grail, whatever our treasure is, is hidden within our own consciousness; it is hidden within our own being—it is there by virtue of our oneness with God. It isn't that it is ours of our own account but because we are joint heirs with Christ in God.

That is only another way of saying, "My oneness with God constitutes my oneness with all spiritual beings and with every spiritual idea or thing." To me that represents one of the highest spiritual statements that I know. I put it in my writing in just that simple language and very seldom does anyone comment on it or say, "You know, I think you've put the Holy Grail there, or the pearl of great price!" They don't recognize it; it seems just a pretty sentence. Actually, I really mean it from the bottom of my heart. To me it ranks as one of the highest statements, one that will put you nearer the realization of heaven on earth than any other.

The highest mystical statement of truth that I know is: "My kingdom is not of this world."[4] I doubt that Jesus said anything of a more mystical nature than that. When he said, "I have overcome the world,"[5] that was, of course, the realization that "My kingdom is not of this world." The statement itself—"My kingdom is not of this world,"—immediately sets us free from the desire of person, place, thing, circumstance or condition; it sets us free from the world of effects and makes us live in conscious union with cause, with God.

You see, if we were to demonstrate millions of effects, we still would be playing around with something that could turn to dust in our hands. But, if once we touch conscious union with cause—or God—then we have no further interest in the things of this world except to enjoy them as they come along. We then are still in the world, but not of it. There is no such thing as a time or a place wherein we would have less than the fullness if we obtain the consciousness that my kingdom is not of this world; if we can see it, hear it, taste it or smell it, but don't get bound up in it.

Don't be concerned about this world—this is the mystical path. Don't be concerned about the flesh—this is the way of the spirit. Don't be too concerned about how it comes out—it is temporary, anyhow. Be concerned with the inner plane of being!

I am going to talk for a few minutes on the two planes—the outer and the inner—because it is on the inner that we make our contact; it is on the outer that we behold humanly the fruitage of it. Of course, it is possible for a person to make his contact on the inner plane, as many ascetics do (many who retire from the world and go to live in monasteries, nunneries and all that), to make that contact on the inner plane and absolutely drop the whole outer world and have no use for it. It is possible, too, to go on and enjoy a wonderful inner life. But somehow for us, that does not seem the natural thing. Personally, I don't think it is quite the right thing except for the few who obtain such heights on that inner plane that they can do more for the world than by mixing in the world.

For most of us, however, what we learn on the inner plane can provide the greatest blessing to those in what we call the outer world. Therefore, we should, until such time as the call comes to leave this world, live in this world. We should share with those of this world all of the depths that are appearing in our inner life.

In my own case there is great enjoyment of the things of the outer world, but there is not a deadly attachment to them that makes me unhappy if I do not have a diamond as big as my neighbor has. (Diamonds, anyway, perhaps are outmoded now—they have found imitations that are better than the real thing! But palaces or yachts, if not diamonds.)

Now, on the inner plane that is within our own being, we touch God, we touch the spiritual identity of all individuals, we touch the spiritual identity of everything that appears as person, place and thing. Touching the reality within makes it manifest to us on the outer, as person, place or thing. It gives us our family, our friends, our students, our patients, our activities; it gives us our books to read. It is a strange thing that every time I touch some new note within me, somebody either presents me with a book, or recommends a book to me, that takes me just a step further, or reveals that point I have found on the inner plane.

In the same way, every time I touch a new thing, a new sense within, it appears outwardly as some new friend or some new helper or some new activity of some kind. It is a very wonderful thing that can't be explained in any other way than that.

Regardless of what business you are in, contact God within yourself and trust that contact to bring to you all that is necessary to your unfoldment. It may not come the day you expect it. As a matter of fact, it may have to come all the way from China so give it a chance to get here! Or the other people in your life may not be in a position just at that moment to become parties to the demonstration. Don't set time limits upon your demonstration. Just find the kingdom of God within your own being. Make that contact and understand that now you are depending on your inner demonstration for your outer expression. You want to make it first on the inner plane and then let the outer plane take care of itself.

I keep repeating to you that the mystical life is one in which you are completely independent of person, place, thing, or activity on the outer plane. Yet, this life is one in which you never are separated from person, place, thing or activity on the outer plane, but where the whole deal is consummated within through your contact with

God, and then brought into visibility as if there was an unseen hand manipulating all the strings.

Now, we are not just metaphysicians who have found some truth that we can hornswoggle into doing our will! Nor have we found some secret means of getting from God what couldn't be gotten in some other way. In other words, we are not making affirmations or denials, but living in conscious realization of God, making God as much a part of our conscious life as Jesus did–that is, if we can. Jesus lived and moved and had his being with only God as the central theme. "I live, yet not I, Christ liveth in me!"[6] There is no more to our outer expressions than what we have realized from the law of our inner fulfillment.

That is the path that we have come on in this work. That's the place where we are headed. Let us watch outwardly that we fulfill our inner duties. I owe nobody here an obligation as a human being, but the mere fact that we're here together means to me that God has brought us. So there is a spiritual demand on me to live so as to present to you a clear and clean consciousness, one devoid of self-interest, one devoid of deception, one devoid of any of the entangling alliances that would separate this message from the creator and the expounder. God is both the creator and the teacher of this message, therefore all those to whom it is entrusted are just what Jesus was to his world–just what every teacher is to his world–the one who is to present that message in its purity, its entirety and its brevity. And, as everyone knows who has taught any subject in the world, it takes clear thinking and clean living to be the right kind of teacher. It requires honesty of purpose. Anybody in the world, now that this is written down, can memorize it and go out and teach it. I doubt very much, though, whether any of the students will benefit greatly by it unless there is spiritual integrity behind it. The words of themselves will raise nobody's consciousness; the words of themselves will not convey an idea of truth. The pages are just so much more black print added to the bookshelves in the world.

It takes the consciousness of an individual inspired, aflame, with love for that in order to impart a spiritual truth, just as it takes a class of people who feel that there is a truth for which they would sacrifice time, money or entertainment or pleasure; in other words, people who are seeking to sit at the feet of the Master. What is the Master? The Master isn't a man; the Master is this divine message, this truth—that's the Master. And to sit at its feet means really to clean up your own consciousness—self-will—selfish desires—to really lay your all on the altar of this truth and say, "Here, everything I have of a material nature all added together isn't worth what even one drop of spiritual truth is worth." In that purified state of consciousness, you would be able to receive and assimilate and respond to the truth of being. How many times has Jesus told us that you've got to leave all for Christ? How many times has he pointed out that this fellow didn't get it because he had to bury his father-in-law, this one had to get married, and this one had to pick his donkey up out of a ditch—or something else? How many have been invited to the feast and couldn't come? Too many other things to do. Too many other obligations. Well, you see, to receive the divine light means to offer one's self on the altar of spiritual truth. It means actually to sacrifice all sense of self, all sense of selfishness or desire for personal gain.

You know, there is no need for the desire for personal gain because in this spiritual truth, what blesses one, blesses all. The more you give, the more you have. And so whether you are at one moment teaching and imparting this spiritual truth, that the more you give the more you have, or whether you are temporarily the student and realize, "The more I give the more I will receive," in both cases it is the same thing.

I have never yet spoken a word or written a word that didn't lift me higher. Why? Because it didn't come out of my brain; it wasn't something I made up. It was an impartation that came from me at the moment that I spoke it and it was just as wonderful to me as it was to anyone who ever heard it. You would know how true this is if you could only be around me as my wife is, or my secretary, when I sometimes read a passage of these things or hear myself say them. I say, "Isn't that marvelous? Isn't that beautiful?" It is—and perhaps I, best of all, can appreciate it because I know the depths out of which it comes. I know the nights of wakefulness. I know the pains that I've gone through.

Right here let me tell you this. This path is not one of roses without thorns! When you decide to make the transition into the mystical life, you will find that you have to give up many of your former concepts of body, of business, of entertainment, of pleasure. You will find new experiences awaiting you. In that period of transition it isn't all harmony. That is why Jesus said, "The way is straight and narrow and few there be that go in thereat."[7]

It really isn't easy in its first stages. As a matter of fact, learning these lessons is apt to be very painful, but many of these lessons only come through suffering, through deep suffering. Without that suffering, we wouldn't learn them. Why? Well, because when we're at peace with the world and all is well, we think everything is going along fine, and we don't really strain, we don't really struggle, we don't really try deep down within ourselves. We just go along and say, "Isn't that good!" Yes, we do! And we don't have our progress.

It is the depth of our trials and tribulations that forces us up, at least for a period. The person who has gone through the most, attains the most not because it is necessary, not because there is any God decreeing it, but because of the word "inertia"—our desire to keep going the way we are going and at the speed we're going. We just love to know that each day is going to be followed by another day of no pain and no lack and no limitation.

No! These great truths—and I've read the lives of many who have gone far on the spiritual path, and I haven't found any one of them who hasn't had his Gethsemane—aren't easy of attainment. If the trials do not come in the form that Jesus faced them, they come in many other forms. It is true, we do not have to go through persecution, we do not have to go through that type of trial, we do not have to stand public condemnation—that all went with olden times and is all out—but we do go through personal and individual strife. It may be within our family; it may be within our community. Somewhere along the line each of us, if we are to catch the depths of this, goes through a period of transition.

If there were no other, there would be this one: The minute you begin to stop depending on persons, right there is a trial when you haven't got that person to lean on as a prop; for instance, when you stop sending out bills to your patients and you are going to depend only on the Christ. That first month when the adjustment is taking place and you just can't ask anybody (and you can't send a bill) I am telling you there is a little period in there when you quake a bit and wonder if it is going to work. It is the same thing when you come to that great place of healing without giving a treatment. Don't think that you haven't got a trial, that you haven't got a River Jordan to cross. You have!

And first comes that temptation, "I don't think I am doing justice to my patients, I don't feel that I am working hard enough." Yes and then comes the second one after some beautiful healings have taken place and the patients have been very generous, and you say, "I can't take this money, I didn't really work for it! I didn't do enough to earn this."

There are all kinds of trials. Those are just the least of them. But there are trials that come with this life. Just think, when you come to that place when you are going to say to yourself, "I really believe that God is the life of all being; therefore, any appearance of error must be nothing more nor less than an hallucination, a temptation, coming to me to believe in a selfhood apart from God. I am just not going to believe it." And then you say to yourself, "Well, that's the treatment." Then you start to remember how you used to think of treatments and then comes your little period of "Aha!"

You'll find it isn't easy. Oh, that's only one of the simplest ones, too. There comes a period when your relations start to tell you that you must have gone crazy. Or your church members will tell you, "Well, you certainly have gone off the beam now!" No. In one way or another there come trials to us either through our own selves, to our family, or to our patients; there come, for awhile, serious problems of health and supply. They come to us in some form—maybe our own, maybe our patients, mostly others—but we have to take charge of them for them and we have to learn to stand very fast. We have to learn to sit up nights with them. We have to learn to go away for forty days. It is going away into the "closet," into our sanctuary, and just praying our heart out, "Let this cup pass from me, but if it doesn't, I can take it on the chin, too!"

Oh, yes, all of these things come on this way—the straight and narrow. Once you give up your reliance on the human means of salvation, once you have chosen this way, you will find that the way is straight and narrow. You find that few there be that go in there and for a while it will almost seem as though you just can't meet anyone who does understand you. I know because I know how many years I not only didn't have the opportunity to talk this way, I didn't have the opportunity to talk in private. Maybe that's why I'm talking so much now. I am just making up for the lost years when I was so silent. I had to be silent because the moment I would speak any of these ideas, people would think I was unbalanced.

If your reliance is on the inner plane, if your reliance is on your contact with God and you feel yourself cut off from dependence on human means of demonstrating your good, there comes a period when you have to sit quietly and secretly within your own being. You have got to work this out without telling the outside world about it. You have got to prove it.

Once you have proven it, the evidence is so great that you don't have to tell it any more except when you are in the process of teaching. You never have to tell anyone that you have found the pearl of great price. In the first place, if you told it, it would be the best evidence available that you hadn't found it. Mainly, though, because it shows in your whole life, in your whole attitude, in your whole being. Everything indicates that you have found it. Then the world wants it. No. They don't want it—they want the fruits of it.

There comes another difficult period for you when you really believe that the world has recognized that you have got it and that it wants it and you want to pour it out. After you have done it for several years (heartbreaking years) you discover they didn't want it at all. They wanted the fruits that they saw you enjoying. That is another reason why you watch your step in this work when someone comes around and says, "Give me that!" You commence to be a little suspicious. Does he really want it? Or does he want the effects, the results? It soon shows up which is which, because if he really wants it, there will be that shown forth that indicates that nothing is so important as that, and all other matters are thrown aside. Then you don't hear, "Well, I can't make it Thursday night, but I'll come Tuesday afternoon. If you can't see me then, I just can't see you!" No, when they want it, they come around and say, "I'll come at midnight if you say so!"

Did you know that Brown-Landone (a noted practitioner) kept office hours all night long? When you made an appointment with him for three o'clock, you had to ask whether it was A.M. or P.M.! I have had many appointments with him at three o'clock in the morning that lasted through until six! Yes. As you get into this work you find that you have no more hours. A.M. or P.M. means absolutely nothing to you except keeping the right record and those who come to you pretty much

can be measured by that very thing. Are they concerned
about whether you want to see them A.M. or P.M. or
Thursday or Friday or Sunday? Because if they are, then
their hearts are not in it.

Let me tell you something: This path isn't for him
whose heart and soul and mind isn't in God. If there is
an idea in your mind at all that this is something which
can be used, that it is something for personal gain, for
personal happiness or personal wealth, don't try it,
because it won't get you anywhere at all. There are too
many good metaphysical systems that can be used just
to bring about personal happiness or personal temporary gains—but this can't. This can bring only immortality and eternality and all the good that God knows. But
it is on an entirely different level than human good, just
as spiritual freedom has nothing to do with human
freedom.

Spiritual freedom, the peace that passeth understanding, isn't dependent on anything in the outer world. It is
dependent on your relationship with the Christ, with
God. As that becomes real, as that becomes embodied,
as it inflames you so that life becomes all in all, you find
yourself living in two worlds: the inner world, the main
one, and the outer world—a pretty good pastime but not
to be taken too seriously and not to be permitted to take
up too much time or effort, the eagerness to get back to
the center is so great.

Probably in my enthusiasm I am giving you the
impression of something abnormal or subnormal about
this way of living. I don't mean that at all. I only mean
that God does become a reality and that we do become
consciously one with it, that it guides every step of our
experience. It supplies us, it draws to us all that we need

in the world—right friendships, right family relationships, right supply, right activity, right books, right clubs—everything that is necessary to advance our cultural and spiritual welfare and provide us with greater opportunity to be of service to the world.

I want to tell you something. I have a deep conviction that for the first time in the history of the entire world spiritual power is going to have something to do with human affairs. I do not believe that at any period up to this present one, God has appeared in the human scene or concerned itself with human problems. I do not believe that if God had been brought anywhere into the human scene that the world would have gone through thousands and thousands of years of wars, tornadoes, earthquakes, famines and pestilence. These things could not have been had God been present in human affairs.

Where has God been in all those years? God is always present in the consciousness of those who are conscious of God's presence. But how many were there? The few who lived in monasteries, the few who lived in ashrams, the few religious students of the world, the few who tried to found religious organizations and failed? Yes, they knew God and they had the benefit of all of God's presence and all of God's power in their individual experience. But it did not come down to the level of the masses. The reason was that spiritual truth has never been given to the world until this present half or three-quarters of a century. All of the religious knowledge of the world was kept for the philosophers and the priests and the rabbis. All that the public ever got were forms and ceremonies and rites and creeds. Never did the Hindu masters teach those who were below the level of the spiritual Brahman. Except for a brief period in

Europe, the period of the Western mystics from about
1200 to 1700 A.D., except for those few centuries, the
masses were never taught spiritual truth. At best Jesus
may have taught it to a few hundred people—just nothing
in the history of the world in numbers. Never has
spiritual consciousness reached the level of mass human
consciousness.

The change began in those years when Christian
Science, Unity and New Thought were given to the
public. The public were encouraged to meditate, ponder, do daily lessons, go to church Wednesday, go to
church Sunday, and then go to church in between to
committee meetings and for daily noon lessons and so
forth and so on. All through the Christian Science era,
the Unity and the New Thought era, this word of God,
this spiritual truth and revelation, has been given to the
public, to the masses, to anyone who would accept it. It
has become a leaven, so that people who do not know
the meaning of the word metaphysics don't say "die"
any more, they say "pass on." Even people who do not
know the meaning of metaphysics talk about disease as
a belief or a claim or admit that there is spiritual power
or admit that diseases have been healed and supply has
been received through metaphysical means or through
spiritual means—even if they themselves know nothing
about it. Doctors admit it because they see cases in the
hospitals. You can't even imagine how many doctors
have come to me in the last few years. As a matter of
fact, today psychosomatic medicine is trying to copy it.
They are seventy years behind the times because they
are now where Christian Science was in 1866, believing
there is a mental cause for a physical disease. They are
back in the days of Rawson—and Mrs. Eddy's early

days—all of these outmoded forms of metaphysics that still believe there is a mental cause for a physical disease.

Why, there *isn't* any disease. You can't have God and a disease, too. There is only one power and that is God. All the rest of it is belief or illusion, whether you call a disease something contracted by infection or by contagion. Back there in those days, however, even though the practice was erroneous, it was a step out of what had been. It took on the language of religion; it brought God into it.

They brought God into it and employed certain forms of consciousness, calling them the Christ, whether it was sub-consciousness, inner-consciousness, super-consciousness, or whatever. They gave fancy names to this thing, but all this had one wonderful effect; it drove people to the subject of God on some other day of the week than Sunday—and it brought people to where they brought God into their daily experience as a means of overcoming their problems.

It doesn't make any difference how crude the beginning was, it had good results—good effect. It spread the word to the world that God wasn't just a Sunday experience and that God wasn't an experience only for the minister, or the priest or the rabbi. God was an experience for you and for me. We could reach conscious oneness with God even if we weren't priests or rabbis.

You don't realize it if you don't think about it; you just can't realize what change took place when God came into the consciousness of the man in the street. It was probably the greatest event that has ever happened in the history of the world. And now for seventy-five years that has been spreading so that just in this little library, for three, four and five periods a day, probably two or three hundred people a day come in here God-conscious. This is only a little tiny spot on the globe. Think how many homes this is carried into from this one center and then multiply that by the Unity centers, the Truth centers, the New Thought centers, and the individual centers and the Christian Science churches, and the Christian Science Reading Rooms; try to multiply all that around the world!

I read the other day that Ralph Waldo Trine's *In Tune with the Infinite* had sold two million copies. Do you know what it would mean for two million people ever to think about God before this era? It was impossible. Now, with this much God in human consciousness—and remember that one grain of God can work miracles—just think with all of this God-consciousness going about through the world how it must be leavening thought, having an influence on our public officials, on our congressmen—all of that! If it hasn't had an influence, it will have, and in increasing degree. The God-consciousness of this world will some day dominate and control the entire consciousness of the world—political, economic, social, as well as religious.

That will come only because for the first time the masses are taking God into their experience and not only seven days a week. We're learning to "pray without ceasing." We are learning to take God into our consciousness even when we sit down for a simple bite of breakfast or lunch. Yes, the thought of the world is being leavened. The thought of the world is being reached with this God-consciousness. It makes no difference which one of these metaphysical movements you think about, each one of them is carrying the word God—the term Christ-consciousness and the idea of God imminent in individual experience—to the world.

So, each one is performing a blessing. Each one is a light unto the world. The day should come when every metaphysical practitioner should be so thoroughly imbued with the Christ that he can heal. And then whether you go to a Christian Science practitioner, or a Unity one, or a New Thought one, or an independent, you will get the same healing. And why?

Let's be honest about this. The teaching has nothing to do with the healing. I don't care if you take all of the metaphysical teachings and tear them up, nothing at all would happen. There would be no effect at all on the healing work, because none of them are correct. Not one of them is right. Not one of them is the pure truth of being—no, not any of them. And if they were, they wouldn't heal! They would only open your consciousness as the part-truth is doing now, the part-truth that is in all of them. They would open your consciousness to the receptivity, to the reception, of the Christ. *That* does the healing!

All of the books out there—thousands of them—won't heal a headache, not even if you could memorize them. The Christ alone is the healer. If there weren't a metaphysical book on earth there is enough truth in the Bible to open consciousness to the Christ. There is enough truth in every one of those metaphysical books out there to open the Christ in consciousness. As little truth as there is in them, there is enough truth to lead us to the Christ—and that is the leavening influence. It isn't the written word that is the leavening influence. "I live, yet not I, Christ liveth in me."

You can go to any metaphysical healer in any of the metaphysical movements and if you find one imbued with the spirit of truth and of Christ, he will heal you, even if he belongs to a movement where the teaching isn't too spiritual. What determines the healing is not the teaching, but the Christ. Please believe me that in every one of the books here there is some measure of the Christ to be found that will open our consciousness to it. But it isn't up to the books and it isn't up to the teachings. The day must come when each practitioner, regardless of his metaphysical background or association, will be so imbued with the Christ that when a call comes the Christ should answer and bring the healing. That's the day that is coming. Places like this open their doors to people of all churches and no churches, to all organizations and no organizations, and make it possible to meet on the common level of Christhood. Nobody can come in here and help the people who come here, except he who is imbued with some measure of that Christ.

That is the mystical way of living—not to be too concerned with the letter of truth, because we have been told over and over again that the "letter killeth." I am not too concerned about these books. I am concerned about the people who read the books, whether they can find in those books some measure of Christ, enough to give them the desire to live it, to carry it out, to carry the thought of God out into this human experience.

Remember somewhere in the Bible that if there are ten righteous men in a town, the town would be saved? There is probably a spiritual law behind that. The chances are that when we get a few tens of righteous people—of God-conscious people, God-intoxicated people if we can—maybe that also will save the town, or the nation, or the world. It can well be, it can very, very well be. It may well be that the righteous thinking of just a few on the inner plane will touch and reach the consciousness of the world.

We have had civilizations wiped out, civilizations that were just as far advanced as this one and some that were further advanced. We probably think that we have the greatest degree of civilization that ever was. No. We are the greatest generation of mechanical engineers but we are not the greatest generation of developed civilization. It was given to other generations to have that honor and they were wiped out and there was no God around stopping it, either. There never will be until God becomes the level of individual and mass consciousness. Then, God works in our human affairs. Remember, God didn't work in your human affairs to any great extent until you caught some glimpse of the Christ and from then on, God governed all of your human affairs. And so today—as God becomes the real consciousness of thousands and thousands and thousands of people, you will find that God-consciousness influencing elections, influencing international work.

That is why we are here. If you think for a moment that we are here just so that we can solve a few of our personal human problems, you don't know the power of the Christ, you don't know the meaning of the Christ. It has nothing to do with just your little personal life or mine. The Christ is a force so tremendous, so great, that when it comes to life, it comes for a universal purpose. Christ is universal good not personal good. Any truth that is individually true is universally true. Therefore, every time there is an individual demonstration of Christ-presence, there is a universal demonstration. It only needs to be recognized on a wider scale. Probably that is why the Bible says that if ten righteous men—not just one or two, but ten—if there is enough leavening of this consciousness, enough spirituality, it will have influence on the other portion of men and states of consciousness.

That doesn't mean that we require numbers. No. One with God is a majority. What it does mean, though, is that enough people are willing to come under the sway of spiritual dominion—that's all, because we cannot with our spirituality bring even the members of our own families into heaven if they don't want to come. That's why the numbers. It just takes a permeating of consciousness, a leavening, so that enough people will want to give up their old human dependency.

I have something that is bothering me right now: "Resist not evil!"[8] Now, as we go out of here watch this carefully. To you who are now active in the work, regardless of the name or nature of your particular problem, stop battling error; so far as you can, try not to fight it too hard. See if you can't take the attitude, "the battle is not yours." Then be still and see the salvation of the Lord. You need not battle. All you have to do is make the acknowledgment that all that is appearing is for the glory of God. See if you can't take this healing work easy. Try to take it as if you really believe that evil isn't a great power.

Supposing right now that you had the personal power to be able to heal a disease—wouldn't if frighten you to death? It should. It should. No, you haven't got that power. The Christ, the infinite invisible, is the only healing agency there is in the world, if you want to call it healing agency. It dispels the illusions of sense—that's all.

On this same subject of mystical power, the great secret is, "I can of my own self do nothing . . . I live, yet not I, Christ liveth in me." And the great secret is not how much personal power can we develop as healers but how good a vehicle are we for Christ, how clear a transparency, what degree of Christ-consciousness are we? In other words, what degree of love for error or hate of error or fear of error is in or out of my consciousness? How much do I really fear error? How much do I really love error? How much do I have error? That is what determines how much a transparency I am, how clear a transparency I am for the Christ—not how much personal power I have got. How clear am I on the great truth that God is no respecter of persons. God is love! In him there is no sin and no disease and we live and move and have our being in Christ-consciousness.

Again, to all of you and to myself, to all of us who are actively engaged in this healing work, watch this activity up in the head. When a call comes, see how much you can stop getting a resistance, a denial, up here in the forehead. That is where it all comes, this resistance. It all rushes in and wants to say, "It isn't true! It isn't true!" See how much we can resist that and actually believe it isn't true! If you really believe it isn't true, you don't have to say it or declare it, you can afford to smile at it. You can afford to see through it and sometimes you may have to keep it up quite a while, the tenacity of error is so strong in some people's thoughts—not that the person is responsible for it, either.

We haven't yet come to the place where we can definitely say why one person can be healed in a minute and another one takes two years. Perhaps some feel like I do that it has to do with pre-existence; it has to do with our history before we made our appearance on this earth plane. I personally believe that. I believe that since life is eternal, we have always lived and since we have always lived, we must have lived in or out of some particular state of consciousness and therefore some are very, very much further developed than others.

If you, this moment, were to pass on, you would not find yourself having to go through all the things you have had to go through until you came to this spiritual awareness. You would very nearly start off where you are this minute as a spiritually developed soul—or very close to it—in some cases, further ahead even because in some cases the act of transition is a freeing one.

Now, there isn't enough clinical proof for anyone to make a definite statement that he knows why one person gets healed quickly and another one doesn't. That is not our particular problem at this moment. Our particular problem is this: the development of the practitioner to that point where he neither fears, hates nor loves error; his development of some measure of Christ-consciousness which means divine love, universal love, a sense of forgiveness, a sense of gratitude, a sense of human affection.

Don't forget that the command of the Master was, "Love thy neighbor."[9] It was not only love God but your neighbor too. You have to love your neighbor as yourself. He gave those two great Commandments. He was most clear that what you had to do was love God *and* love your neighbor. You know, we get so absolute about our love for God sometimes that we just forget our neighbor. But we don't want to do that in this work. We want to take the full measure of the Christ. We want to love God with all our heart and with all our soul but we want to love our neighbor, too. And we want to show forth that love in compassion, in patience, in justice, in kindness, in forbearance, in joy—in willingness to share all of the good that God has given us. Above all we want to give up our egotistic belief that we have personal powers as practitioners. Our healings will be in proportion as we realize that all power is given to me through God, through Christ which strengtheneth me. That is the only source of our power.

That idea of no personal power comes in, you remember, in this idea of leading the spiritual life or mystical life where we are not dependent on person, place or thing by our outer contact, but we are dependent on the inner plane, on our inner contact with God. Now, this probably is the closing. Here is the method, if there be any method, to demonstration. Contact the Father within. Gain the conscious realization of the presence and power of God *within* your own being. Regardless of the name or nature of the problem or need, don't try to solve it as that. Don't try to solve supply as supply. Don't try to solve family relations as family relations. Drop all thought of them. Go within until you actually find that place within your being which gives you the God-response—and then you solve your problems! Once you have touched the Christ within your own being, you have touched every phase of your demonstration. Conscious oneness with God! This constitutes conscious oneness with all spiritual being and with every spiritual idea!

SCRIPTURAL REFERENCES

Chapter 1
1. Psalms 127:1.
2. John 18:36.
3. John 5:30.
4. Galatians 2:20.

Chapter 2
1. John 16:7.
2. John 10:27.
3. John 10:30.
4. John 16:15.
5. Exodus 20:13.
6. John 12:32.
7. John 5:30.
8. Galatians 2:20.
9. Exodus 20:3.
10. John 19:11.
11. John 14:6.
12. Matthew 6:33.
13. John 8:58.
14. Matthew 28:20.
15. Matthew 18:20.
16. Psalms 46:10.
17. I Kings 19:12.

Chapter 3
1. Matthew 6:25.
2. Matthew 6:32.
3. Matthew 6:27.
4. Isaiah 55:8.
5. John 9:3.
6. John 10:27.
7. Zechariah 4:6.
8. John 8:58.
9. Matthew 28:20.
10. John 16:7.
11. Galatians 2:20.
12. Exodus 20:5.
13. Jeremiah 31:29.
14. John 14:6.

Chapter 4
1. Matthew 28:20.
2. John 18:36.
3. Matthew 6:25.
4. Matthew 26:39.
5. Zechariah 4:6.

Chapter 5
1. Luke 15:31.
2. Psalms 91:7.
3. Matthew 16:23.

Chapter 6
1. John 10:30.
2. Matthew 5:25.
3. John 18:36.
4. Isaiah 26:3.
5. Zechariah 4:6.
6. Matthew 11:15.
7. Matthew 4:4.
8. John 6:49.
9. John 6:58.

Chapter 7
1. I Kings 19:12.
2. John 16:15.
3. Matthew 7:12.

Chapter 8
1. John 18:36.
2. John 16:33.
3. Matthew 26:40.
4. John 16:7.

Chapter 9
1. John 10:30.
2. Matthew 6:25.
3. Luke 12:32.
4. Psalms 23:2.
5. John 16:33.
6. John 14:9.
7. Matthew 11:3.
8. Matthew 11:4.
9. John 10:30, Luke 15:31.
10. Romans 8:17.
11. Luke 15:31.
12. Matthew 28:20.
13. Isaiah 43:2.

Chapter 10
1. Matthew 7:12.
2. Matthew 25:36.
3. Matthew 6:27.
4. Matthew 6:25.
5. John 5:8.
6. John 16:15.
7. I Samuel 3:9.
8. Psalms 46:10.
9. John 5:30.
10. John 5:31.
11. John 7:16.
12. Galatians 2:20.

Chapter 11
1. John 5:30.

Chapter 12
1. Isaiah 26:3.
2. John 10:30.
3. John 16:15.
4. John 10:27.
5. John 18:36.
6. John 4:32.
7. John 16:33.
8. John 14:10.
9. Psalms 91:7.

Chapter 13
1. John 18:36.   2. Matthew 6:33.

Chapter 16
1. Philippians 2:5.   4. Matthew 12:13.
2. Matthew 4:4.   5. John 5:8.
3. Matthew 5:25.   6. John 19:11.

Chapter 17
1. I Samuel 3:9.   6. Isaiah 26:3.
2. I Kings 19:12.   7. Matthew 5:39.
3. Psalms 46:10.   8. II Chronicles 20:17.
4. Matthew 6:33.   9. II Chronicles 20:15.
5. John 10:30.   10. John 4:32.

Chapter 18
1. John 10:10.   6. Galatians 2:20.
2. Matthew 6:33.   7. Matthew 7:14.
3. John 16:7.   8. Matthew 5:39.
4. John 18:36.   9. Matthew 19:19.
5. John 16:33.